Minute WONDERS of the WORLD

Minute WONDERS of *the* WORLD

by

ALFRED SKRENDA

AND

ISABEL JUERGENS

∿

"*I speak of that learning which makes us acquainted with the boundless extent of nature, and the universe, and which even while we remain in the world, discovers to us both heaven, earth, and sea.*"   —CICERO

∿

GROSSET & DUNLAP
Publishers
NEW YORK

FOREWORD

IT IS interesting to know that the *septem mira* (seven wonders of the world) of ancient times were all confined to the creations of man. They were the Pyramids of Egypt, the Gardens of Semiramis (Hanging Gardens of Babylon), the Statue of Jupiter at Olympia, the Temple of Diana at Ephesus, the Tomb of Mausolus at Halicarnassus, the Pharos at Alexandria, and the Colossus of Rhodes.

The people of the Middle Ages also selected seven works of man, namely, the Colosseum of Rome, the Catacombs of Alexandria, the Great Wall of China, Stonehenge, the Leaning Tower of Pisa, the Porcelain Tower of Nanking, and the Mosque of St. Sophia at Constantinople as the seven marvels of their world.

In our time we are more inclined to pay tribute to the wonders of nature as well as the creations of man the builder. Prompted by local pride, every corner of the world hopefully adds its "eighth wonder" in the form of a cataract, or a cavern, or a bridge, or a tower, and with the ease and popularity of travel today, millions of people migrate to and fro to gaze upon these many wondrous sights and places.

From the thousands of awe-inspiring works of God and man upon the surface of the globe, we have selected 144 and have attempted to describe them with brief text and drawings in our little book. Many of these you may have visited, and our pages may refresh your memories of their beauty and grandeur. Others, tucked away in far-away places, we may be unveiling for you for the first time.

One of Shakespeare's characters says: "Why, then the world's mine oyster, which I with sword will open." The world *is* our oyster! We should all strive to see as many of its marvels as we can during our lifetime, or if it be not our good fortune to visit them, let us learn to know more about them through the pages of a book. It is with the idea of making familiar to all as many of the world's wonders as is possible within the physical confines of this book that we have collaborated in MINUTE WONDERS OF THE WORLD.

ALFRED SKRENDA
ISABEL JUERGENS

CONTENTS

South America

Europe

View from the west showing the main entrance.

THE ADLER PLANETARIUM

THE Adler Planetarium and Astronomical Museum is housed in a beautiful edifice, with the signs of the Zodiac sculptured on the twelve sides which surround its dome. A wide corridor encircling its central hall contains the museum, historical instruments and documents, working models of observatories and telescopes, spectroscopes, navigation instruments, and all the paraphernalia necessary to carry on astronomical research and explain it to the layman.

The Planetarium itself, where astronomy is dramatized against a huge dome representing the heavens, occupies the center hall, 70 feet in diameter. There the stars, the great galaxy, the planets, the nebulae, and clusters are so perfectly reproduced that one forgets being indoors and gains the illusion of gazing into the wide spaces of the starlit sky.

Behind the scenes a grotesque instrument on steel stilts with innumerable lenses projects the action of the solar system on the dome, while electric motors move the heavenly bodies.

Cycles requiring centuries can be reproduced in as many minutes. Different aspects of the sky from different parts of the earth can be shown on request, such as the increasing elevation of the Polar Star as one journeys northward, or the Southern Hemisphere with the Southern Cross high in the heavens. One may even see the sky of the distant future when Vega will point out the North Pole.

BONE CABIN QUARRY, Wyoming

FOSSILIZED FISH FROM ONE OF THE QUARRIES

DURING the last fifty years three important types of quarries have been discovered in eastern Wyoming. The first is the fossil fish quarry near Sherman, where seas which dried ages ago have left strange prehistoric fish embedded in the clay, hardened like bas-reliefs.

Then the paleontologists discovered great strata filled with bones of giant creatures of the earliest geological ages, often quite complete skeletons of huge birds, of forest mammoths, and most interesting, of the monsters, half-reptile and half-fish or bird, which dwelt in the marshy shores of the receding seas of prehistoric days.

The third and largest quarries record the habits of the first men who emerged as the ages passed. There were quantities of quartzite and jasper here, and evidently these primi-

tive peoples chipped themselves arrowheads and knives and tools from these stones.

In a plain nearby have been found innumerable circles of stones for anchoring hide wigwam covers, left from their encampments.

The quarries from which they chipped their tools were in the sides of steep cliffs, and they worked along fissures where water had settled and frozen, cracking out the quartz, flint, and moss agate for them. Stone seats and anvils in the side of the cliff show where the primitive artisans sat and shaped their tools. Quantities of scrapers, drills, and heavy hammer stones showing hard usage lie discarded nearby.

These three quarries constitute one of the richest storehouses of prehistoric remains in the world.

UNDER CONSTRUCTION

The BOULDER DAM

WHEN Boulder Dam is completed in 1938, it will represent the most imposing engineering feat ever undertaken by man. Located on the Colorado River between northwestern Arizona and southeastern Nevada, this great concrete horseshoe, 1180 feet long and 727 feet from foundation to crest, will be the highest dam in the world. The 1328 billion cubic feet of water it will impound (two years' flow of the mighty Colorado) will create the largest artificial lake in existence, 115 miles long, 600 feet deep, and with a shoreline of over 500 miles. This water will supply baths for the citizens of far-away Los An-

geles, more electric power than Niagara and Muscle Shoals combined can develop, and both irrigation and flood protection for the Imperial Valley below.

Three and one-half million cubic yards of concrete will be required to complete this giant plug to a river which drains an area three times the size of Germany. Before construction could begin, it was necessary to "bypass" the river at the point selected for the dam site. Four tunnels drilled through the solid rock on each side of the canyon divert it from its age-old bed. Later, when the dam is completed, these bores will be "plugged" and the turbid waters of one of the earth's wildest rivers will forever be tamed. Smaller tunnels, 50 feet in diameter, will carry off flood waters and water for irrigation purposes.

The cost of the dam and reclamation work is estimated at $165,000,-000.

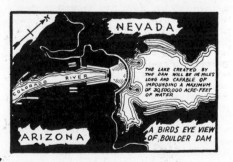

NEVADA

THE LAKE CREATED BY THE DAM WILL BE 115 MILES LONG AND CAPABLE OF IMPOUNDING A MAXIMUM OF 30,500,000 ACRE-FEET OF WATER

COLORADO RIVER

ARIZONA

A BIRDS EYE VIEW OF BOULDER DAM

FROM THE NORTHEAST

The UNITED STATES CAPITOL

laid the corner stone on September 18, 1793.

TO L'ENFANT, the young engineer appointed by President Washington to lay out a Federal City on the banks of the Potomac, Capitol Hill, rising 90 feet above tidewater, seemed like "a pedestal waiting for its monument." The vast pile, 751 feet in length and 350 feet in width, which crowns it today, is perhaps the most imposing of all the national capitols.

In the competition which was held to select a suitable design, two architects, Stephen Hallett and William Thornton, divided the first prize—$500 and a building lot—and under their direction construction began in 1793. President Washington, himself,

Scarcely had the two sandstone wings (on either side of the present rotunda) connected by a wooden shelter been completed, when the British applied the torch to them in 1814. On the Fourth of July, 1851, President Fillmore laid the corner stone of the great north and south marble wings, one to accommodate the Senate, the other the House of Representatives, and in the midst of the War between the States the noble cast-iron dome was completed and the majestic bronze statue of "Freedom" was placed upon its pinnacle, 287 feet above the east base line. The guide tells the visitor who gazes up into the lofty dome that the distance from the floor to the roof is 135 feet, and that beneath the floor on which he stands is the unused crypt once intended to hold the coffin of the first President.

The Armory—Shinav's Wigwam

The CARLSBAD CAVERNS

MEN have explored the regions around the North and South Poles, but the famous Carlsbad Caverns down in southeastern New Mexico still remain only partly explored. Each year new passages are found, until today some eight miles of corridors, chambers, and underground palaces with fantastic chandeliers of vari-colored stalactites and stalagmite domes often 60 feet high are open to the public. This series of caverns dwarfs any other example of subterranean erosion in the world. To assure the preservation of this great natural wonder, a National Park comprising 193 square miles was created in 1930.

It is said that the Carlsbad Caverns were first discovered in 1901 by two cowboys, Jim White and Abijah Long, who thought they saw smoke issuing from a hole in the ground one day at sundown. The "smoke" proved to be millions of bats which emerge each evening during the summer months from the cave.

The limestone decorations of these caves are truly marvelous in their coloring and dimensions. The dome of the Big Room is 15,000 feet around and rises 500 feet from the floor. This room, itself, is almost a mile long. Many of the chambers and galleries lie 1000 feet below the surface, where the temperature remains at 56 degrees Fahrenheit the year round.

The CITADEL of LA FERRIÈRE, Haiti

LONG years of violence and bloodshed in Haiti climaxed in the tyrannical reign (1811–1820) of "King" Christophe, the slave boy from Granada. He was constantly haunted by fear that the peasants whom he forced to work for him, or the French whom they had driven out, or Pétion, the mulatto ruler of the South, would attack him, and he began feverishly to construct a citadel on the highest, most inaccessible peak on the island. It was a terrific task, for all stone and guns and materials had to be dragged up a killing climb in the tropic heat. Ten thousand out of that small population died in the work. Even women and children were forced to trundle sand and carry stones.

The hulking prow of the citadel rises on the pinnacle of the mountain. Its loneliness, its size and solidity, are tremendous, and such a gigantic task could never have been accomplished by those easy-going natives had they not been driven by lashes and an overwhelming fear of the narrow cells of the dungeon where men were lowered without food and water to a slow death.

When, one hot day, paralysis struck down Christophe and he shot himself, his followers swung his body in a hammock up the steep trail to La Ferrière, and to prevent its desecration, immersed it in the lime pit. Thus the "King" finally abode in that amazing citadel of which he said in bitter pride, "Nowhere else can a black man hold up his head."

CLEOPATRA'S NEEDLE

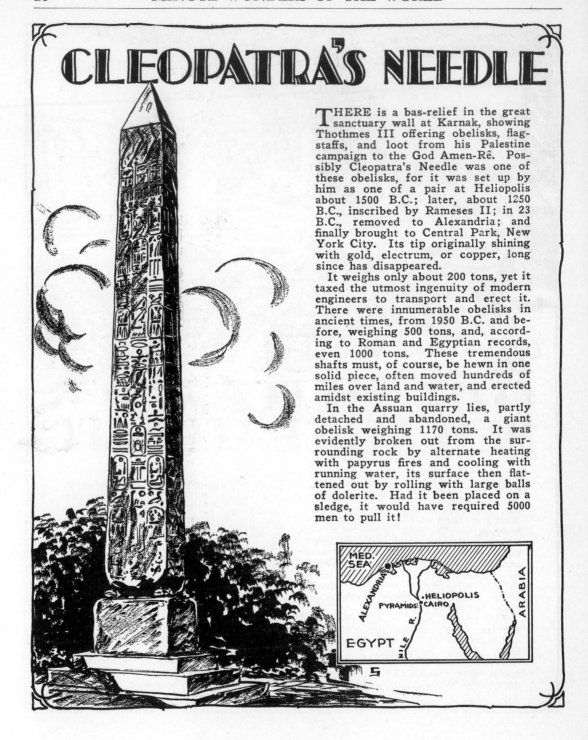

THERE is a bas-relief in the great sanctuary wall at Karnak, showing Thothmes III offering obelisks, flag-staffs, and loot from his Palestine campaign to the God Amen-Rê. Possibly Cleopatra's Needle was one of these obelisks, for it was set up by him as one of a pair at Heliopolis about 1500 B.C.; later, about 1250 B.C., inscribed by Rameses II; in 23 B.C., removed to Alexandria; and finally brought to Central Park, New York City. Its tip originally shining with gold, electrum, or copper, long since has disappeared.

It weighs only about 200 tons, yet it taxed the utmost ingenuity of modern engineers to transport and erect it. There were innumerable obelisks in ancient times, from 1950 B.C. and before, weighing 500 tons, and, according to Roman and Egyptian records, even 1000 tons. These tremendous shafts must, of course, be hewn in one solid piece, often moved hundreds of miles over land and water, and erected amidst existing buildings.

In the Assuan quarry lies, partly detached and abandoned, a giant obelisk weighing 1170 tons. It was evidently broken out from the surrounding rock by alternate heating with papyrus fires and cooling with running water, its surface then flattened out by rolling with large balls of dolerite. Had it been placed on a sledge, it would have required 5000 men to pull it!

WYOMING   NEB.
UTAH COLORADO
KAN
o MESA VERDE
ARIZ. NEW MEXICO

The CLIFF PALACE at MESA VERDE, COLORADO

CLIFF PALACE, most extensive building of the Cliff Dwellers, is an immense ruined castle perched dizzily on the side of a precipice overhanging the San Juan River basin. It was half natural cave and half hewn out of the rock, its innumerable cells and narrow-ledged terraces reached by winding carved steps where a shower of stone arrows from above could send any enemy crashing to death far below.

The ground floor of the Palace is 400 feet long and sometimes 80 wide, and contains 117 rooms. There are four stories in places, and many isolated rooms dug out in inaccessible spots, once reached by ropes or ladders. On the shallow open terraces were fireplaces, and also in some of the rooms whose colored dados are blackened with smoke, for there were no chimneys. The doorways were often T-shaped, the narrow part for the legs and the wider upper part to permit a bundle of wood to be carried through.

The dry air has preserved all wonderfully, for though the Cliff people left probably 500 years ago, there are beautiful jars and pottery, warm winter clothes of cotton lined with turkey feathers, baskets and sandals woven of yucca, and many roof timbers painfully chipped out from far-off trees by stone axes and dragged to this mid-air perch, no one knows how.

WASH.
PACIFIC OCEAN
OREGON
■ CRATER LAKE
CAL.   NEV.

Glacier Pk.   Llao Rock   Timber Crater   Sentinel   Cloud cap   Scott Pk.
The Watchman   Grouse Hill   Rock
            Wizard Is.

DIAGRAM OF CRATER LAKE AND SURROUNDING PEAKS.

The Phantom Ship

CRATER LAKE

IN SOME ancient time there rose in what are now known as the Cascade Mountains of southwestern Oregon a peak which geologists call Mount Mazama, whose crest must have reached an elevation as high as that of Mount Rainier. As the result of some tremendous cataclysm, the entire upper part of this great mountain was either blown off, or it sank into the bowels of the earth, leaving a vast hole, or crater, which gradually filled with clear spring water to its present depth of 2000 feet.

On all sides of this beautiful lake, which is six miles in diameter and whose waters vary from a delicate turquoise to a deep Prussian blue, the walls of the crater rise a sheer 1000 feet, and are formed of fantastically contorted lava. The surface of the lake is 6177 feet above sea level. So far, it has no known outlet, though its waters, which remain at a constant level, may escape by subterranean channels into the Klamath River.

In the midst of Crater Lake is an island, called Wizard Island, where one may see miniature craters and strange lava formations. Another smaller island is called the Phantom Ship, whose outlines suggest a ship under full sail. In certain slants of light the Phantom Ship suddenly disappears.

Crater Lake and the surrounding area of 250 square miles now comprise a National Park. The Klamath and Modoc Indians, because of the mystery and wonder of this strange geological formation, believed that the lake held the throne of their god Llao.

The EMPIRE STATE BUILDING

THE tallest man-made structure in the world, a $50,000,000 miracle of steel, brick, limestone, granite, marble, glass, chromium, and aluminum, stood ready for 25,000 tenants to move into on the site which 20 months before the old Waldorf-Astoria Hotel had occupied.

The Empire State Building rises 1248 feet (nearly a quarter of a mile!) from sidewalk to aviation beacon. Its ground floor covers two acres on Fifth Avenue between Thirty-third and Thirty-fourth Streets in New York City. After the fifth story there is a setback of 60 feet, from which point the king of skyscrapers rises a sheer 1000 feet to that unique, crowning feature of modernity, the mooring mast for aircraft, a 200-foot tower of steel, so rigidly braced that it can withstand a jolt of 50 tons.

Vertical bands of nickel-steel, together with plates of aluminum between the windows, add to the effect of sheerness and height. Its architects have computed that this giant structure weighs no more than a 45-foot rock pile covering the same site. So evenly is its load distributed on its 200 steel columns that it might have been many stories higher than its present 102 floors, had it been economically feasible.

The GARDEN of the GODS, COLORADO

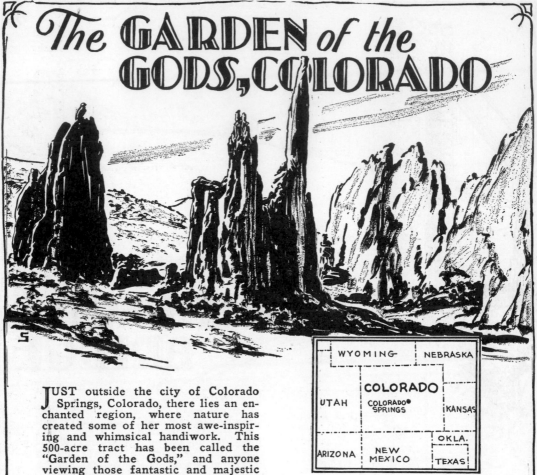

JUST outside the city of Colorado Springs, Colorado, there lies an enchanted region, where nature has created some of her most awe-inspiring and whimsical handiwork. This 500-acre tract has been called the "Garden of the Gods," and anyone viewing those fantastic and majestic monuments carved by the winds and rains and frosts of thousands of centuries out of the strata of red and white sandstone will say that it has most fittingly been named.

One comes first to the Gateway of the Garden, whose blood-red pillars rise 330 feet above the plain. Through them one has a noble vista of snow-capped Pike's Peak, towering nearly three miles into the sky. And now one finds himself in a fairyland of gorgeously colored sculptured stone—of elephants, gargoyles, sphinxes, giant toadstools—all whimsies of Mother Nature and her handmaidens, the wind and the water.

Most impressive of all of the Garden's natural monuments are the "Cathedral Spires," whose slender and graceful steeples reach a height of 250 feet. Nearby is Cathedral Rock, beautiful in its sheer, unadorned majesty. Not even the hand of man could fashion a more massive and romantic pile than the "Tower of Babel," looming nearly 300 feet above the landscape. A short distance away is the Balanced Rock, as "big as a barn," looking as though a child might push it over, but "all the king's horses" could not pull it down.

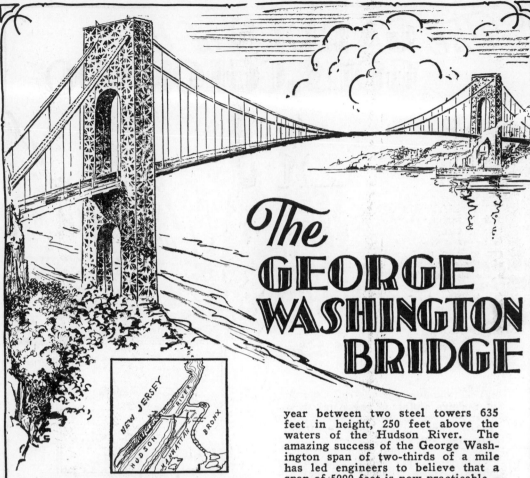

The GEORGE WASHINGTON BRIDGE

THE first suspension bridge in the United States was a 72-foot span built in the year 1796 at Uniontown, Pa. Since then there has been unbelievable progress in bridges swung from cables, climaxing in the 3500-foot span of the George Washington bridge, opened in the fall of 1931 to connect upper Manhattan Island with New Jersey at Fort Lee.

This development was chiefly due to the engineering genius of John A. Roebling. His discovery of spinning thousands of steel wires into gigantic cables three feet thick makes it possible to swing a roadway capable of carrying 45,000,000 automobiles each year between two steel towers 635 feet in height, 250 feet above the waters of the Hudson River. The amazing success of the George Washington span of two-thirds of a mile has led engineers to believe that a span of 5000 feet is now practicable.

This great crossing, named in honor of the first President in the year of the bicentennial celebration of his birth, was begun in May, 1927. Including the land used for the elaborate approaches and ramps at either end, the cost was over $60,000,000. The total length, including approaches, is 8700 feet. The upper deck bears eight traffic lanes in addition to wide foot paths. Provision is made for a lower deck to carry rapid transit lines.

Few people know that the expansion caused by the heat brings the center of the great span twelve feet nearer the water in the summer than in the winter.

The GRAND CANYON of the COLORADO

NO MATTER what extravagant descriptions one has heard of the Grand Canyon, the actual sight of it is never a disappointment. It is too stupendous, too thrilling, and too constantly changing to be compassed by mere words.

Through a great plateau stretching from Arizona into Utah, the Colorado River has been working for ages to chisel itself a swifter channel to the sea—dredging, carving, polishing, sculpturing for 10,000,000 years or so, since the glaciers melted from North America and streams began to slip away to the ocean.

Now, as one looks down from the rim of the canyon, the great river flows, a tiny yellow thread a mile below in a gorge where towering granite walls reflect a thousand brilliant colors, carmine, maroon, burnt umber, pink, amethyst—all changing from moment to moment as the light varies and the sun passes overhead.

The weird rock carvings, gargoyles, pinnacles, cornices, cast ever-shifting shadows over the kaleidoscopic range of that earthbound sunset of colors, 56 miles long.

The vast quantity of soil particles which the water has dredged out in its millions of years of constant flowing is deposited in the immense and fertile Imperial Valley. Today the irresistible river is still interminably at work and an average of 1,000,000 tons of sand and silt pass a given point every 24 hours, while the Colorado continually adds to that record of geological ages carved in the iridescent walls of the Grand Canyon.

The GREAT LAKES

Grain Elevators—
a familiar sight on
the Great Lakes.

WHEN De Champlain set out from Quebec in 1615 to explore what we now know as the Great Lakes, he did not dream that those five bodies of fresh water one day would become the most important inland transportation system in all the world. Lakes Superior, Huron, Michigan, Erie, and Ontario, named in order of their area, together with their connecting links, St. Mary's River, the Straits of Mackinac, St. Clair River and Lake, Detroit River, and Niagara River, constitute a great inland sea stretching 1160 miles from the western tip of Superior to the St. Lawrence River.

With a drainage area of 300,000 square miles (60 per cent of which lies within the boundaries of the United States) and a coast line of over 3000 miles, they have a water surface of 96,000 square miles. Lake Superior, largest of the five, lies 600 feet above sea level. From this level to that of Lake Erie the fall is only 30 feet, but between Erie and Ontario there is a drop of 320 feet, chiefly accounted for by the Falls of the Niagara. The deepest recorded soundings are in Superior—1180 feet. Erie is the shallowest of all the lakes.

For the iron ore beds of Minnesota, the copper mines of Michigan, and the rich fruit and grain farms of the lower lake regions, the Great Lakes supply cheap and easy transportation, with the result that their influence upon the economic growth of North America has been tremendous.

The GREAT SALT LAKE

A swimmer cannot possibly sink in the Great Salt Lake

DURING the last million years, when the glaciers melted away from what is now Utah, they left a giant inland sea over the entire northern part of the state. This was later called Lake Bonneville, after the explorer who in 1835 traced its one-time beaches in the gravel and rocks where he found fossils of strange shrimps and prehistoric fish which had flourished there.

Lake Bonneville has been evaporating for thousands of years, and now all that is left of it is the Great Salt Lake, about 75 miles long and 30 to 50 miles wide, only one-tenth the size of the original lake.

The Jordan, Weber, and Bear Rivers flow into the low basin which holds the lake, bringing in their apparently fresh water myriads of mineral and salt particles from the earth through which they have passed. These atoms collect constantly, and as the lake is so low that it has no outlet to carry them away and keep its water changed and freshened, it grows steadily brinier, until now it is three and one-half times as salt as the ocean. It is so saline that a swimmer cannot possibly sink in it.

It was to the lonely shores of this lake that Brigham Young led his band of Mormons in 1847, seeking a sanctuary. Here they built up a wealthy community, and their impressive Tabernacle still dominates this strange lake which holds the saltiest water in the world.

The GREAT SERPENT MOUND

IN THE vast territory which stretches from the Canadian border south to the Gulf of Mexico may be found today a great number of mounds which are believed to have been constructed by the ancestors of the American Indians. Presenting a wide variety of shapes and sizes, conical, square-based, in the form of gigantic birds, reptiles, and mammals, these strange earthen structures, many of them from 500 to 1000 feet in length, were in some way connected with the tribal totems and religious ceremonies of their builders.

One of the largest Indian mounds, the Great Serpent Mound, lies in Adams County, Ohio, stretching for 1350 feet along a narrow ridge at the junction of two streams. Its situation leads one to believe that it was constructed as a defensive work, though it might also have had a religious significance. Across the widely-opened jaws the Great Serpent measures 75 feet. The body, itself, is 30 feet across and 5 feet high. The loops form circular, fort-like enclosures, surrounded by earthen walls. The strange monster ends up with a tail in the form of a triple coil.

Many of the mounds, when opened, are found to contain skeletons, and so must have served as tribal burial places. Indian races were still occupying mounds, and even constructing them, as late as a century after the discovery of America.

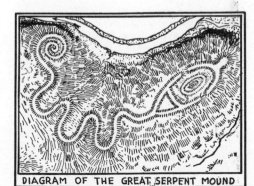

DIAGRAM OF THE GREAT SERPENT MOUND

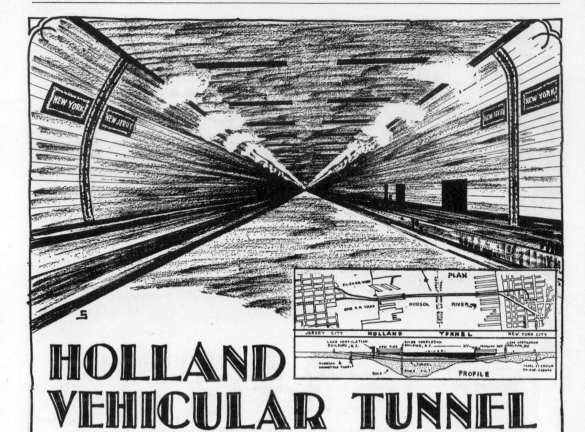

HOLLAND VEHICULAR TUNNEL

THE twin vehicular tubes, passing beneath the busy waters of the Hudson (or North) River between Manhattan Island and New Jersey, were named after the brilliant engineer, Clifford M. Holland, who designed them but never lived to see them completed. The boring of the two tubes, each 29 feet in diameter, and each containing two brightly lighted, white-tile-lined traffic lanes, so well ventilated by giant blowers situated at each terminus that the air is almost as fresh as on any outside motor highway, is considered one of the greatest engineering feats of all time.

Seven years after work had commenced on the 9250-foot tunnel, it was opened for traffic on November 13, 1927, and that day 180,000 passengers in 50,000 vehicles passed through the east- and west-bound tubes. Built to accommodate 46,000 vehicles a day, that figure often has been exceeded.

As the motorist speeds through the shining white tunnel (it requires only six minutes to negotiate the mile and three-quarters from entrance to exit), he very probably does not think of the painfully slow process during those seven years of construction, when the great shields in which the men worked far down below the floor of the river, moving inch by inch from both sides, ate their way through the bedrock to the spot where they would meet in the middle.

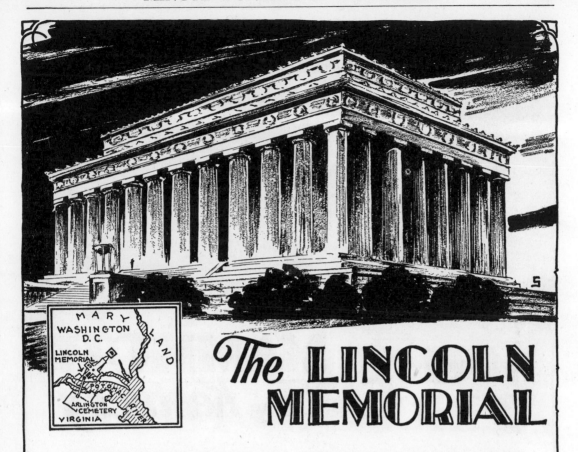

MARYLAND
WASHINGTON
D. C.
LINCOLN
MEMORIAL
POTOMAC
ARLINGTON
CEMETERY
VIRGINIA

The LINCOLN MEMORIAL

IN ALL the world there stands no more beautiful temple erected in memory of a man than that classic building on the banks of the Potomac River in Washington, on the axis formed by the Capitol and the Washington Monument—the Lincoln Memorial.

Built of Colorado marble, Indiana limestone, and Massachusetts granite, the memorial to Abraham Lincoln, which takes the general form of an ancient Greek temple, was begun on February 12, 1914, and completed, at a cost of more than two and a half million dollars. It is 202 feet long by 132 feet wide, and the attic is 80 feet from the top of the foundations. It consists of one large oblong enclosed hall, surrounded by a colonnade of Doric columns, representing the states of the Union. Just inside the hall, opposite the entrance, is the heroic seated statue of Lincoln, carved out of Georgia marble by Daniel Chester French. On the walls of the hall are memorial tablets bearing Lincoln's second inaugural speech and his Gettysburg address, over which are the famous Guerin murals.

The gleaming white of the Memorial, together with the stately approaches and noble flights of steps, and the green of its boxwood and smooth lawns, are mirrored in the artificial lagoons which extend eastward toward the austere shaft of the Washington Monument.

Mammoth Dome

MAMMOTH CAVE, Kentucky

MAMMOTH CAVE is but one of more than 500 explored caverns which exist in the layer of limestone covering that region of Kentucky. All of them are the work of subterranean waters seeking drainage into the Wolin, Green, and Barren Rivers, and their passages extend for thousands of miles.

There is not space here to describe the miles of stately halls and avenues and chambers lined with stalactites and stalagmites, their vaulted roofs of sparkling white limestone encrusted with crystals of black gypsum and nodules of flint, nor the underground rivers in whose clear waters the eyeless fish have never seen the light of day, nor the subterranean waterfalls and natural bridges, which are but a few of the wonders of this remarkable cave.

Just a word, however, about Mammoth Dome, one of the three major domes of the cavern, a natural cathedral 400 feet long, 150 feet high, and 150 feet wide, whose walls of white stone look like folded drapery, whose ceiling is supported by fluted columns 25 feet thick and 80 feet high, whose floor is paved with limestone stained red and black by oxidation. Here the Indians used to gather long before the day of the white man, in quest of flint for their arrowheads.

Visitors to the cave are struck by the pure, exhilarating air which blows through its miles of corridors, making the outside air seem flat and heavy by contrast.

Castillo - the temple of the Mayan God Kukul Can.

The MAYA Marvels of Central America

IN THE fertile valley of the Copan River in Honduras are innumerable stone relics of a civilization that flourished there from 11 B.C. to 340 A.D., then suddenly and unaccountably abandoned the spot and scattered northward, to leave traces by various lakes and rivers, finally culminating in the later Yucatan marvels at Chichén Itzá.

The monoliths, elaborately and deeply carved by the means of flint chisels, the bas-reliefs, among the finest in the world, the grimly realistic portrayals of barbaric gods—all indicate a civilization which had progressed through generations. The stone figures wear beautiful textiles and fine jewelry, woven sandals and intricate anklets, yet no remains of these have been found. Their hieroglyphs evidently repeat a detailed history; so far no archæologist has deciphered them.

Chichén Itzá in Yucatan, where the mysteriously dispersed Central Americans finally settled, is a great plaza with subterranean rivers providing continuous water. The Spaniards in 1517 destroyed as much as possible of the impious Mayan works. But the massive temple pyramids of dazzling white limestone, square and flat-roofed, richly carved, approached by flights of steps, covered with brightly painted reliefs, still stand in impressive groups, a veritable city of them, their ornamented solidity testifying to the expertness of their builders.

THE PROCESSIONAL WAY TO THE GREAT CENOTE OF SACRIFICE, DOWN WHICH YOUNG MAIDENS WERE LED TO THE SACRED POOL. THESE YOUNG GIRLS WERE SACRIFICED TO THE RAIN GOD.

DIAGRAM OF CHICHÉN ITZÁ - YUCATAN

The 100-Inch Telescope ~

MOUNT WILSON OBSERVATORY

AS FAR back as ancient Babylonian days, a temple was built in the city of Babylon for astronomical purposes, while in 2300 B.C. the Chinese built observatories in which to measure the height of the sun. The Greeks, too, at Alexandria in 300 B.C., and later the Persians, at Maragha, erected temples where they could chart the stars. The first prototype of the modern observatory, however, was that of Tycho Brahe on the island of Hveen, Denmark, begun in the year 1576. When the telescope was invented in 1609, rapid strides were made in the science of astronomy, and the need for specially equipped observatories became pressing.

The first observatory in America was established at Chapel Hill, N. C., in 1831, but was destroyed by fire seven years later. Some famous ones of today are the Lick Observatory, on Mount Hamilton, Cal., and the Yerkes Observatory at Williams Bay, Wis. But the observatory which houses the largest reflecting telescope in the world is the Carnegie Solar Observatory, built in 1905 on Mount Wilson, 5700 feet above sea level, near Pasadena, Cal.

Here also is a tower telescope, 150 feet high, wherewith, by means of mirrors, sunlight is reflected down a tube into a vertical spectroscope below. The huge, sliding dome housing the 100-inch Hooker reflector (work has also begun upon a mighty 200-inch reflector), stands on the mountain top, while the laboratories are located in Pasadena, down in the valley below.

The NATURAL BRIDGE of VIRGINIA

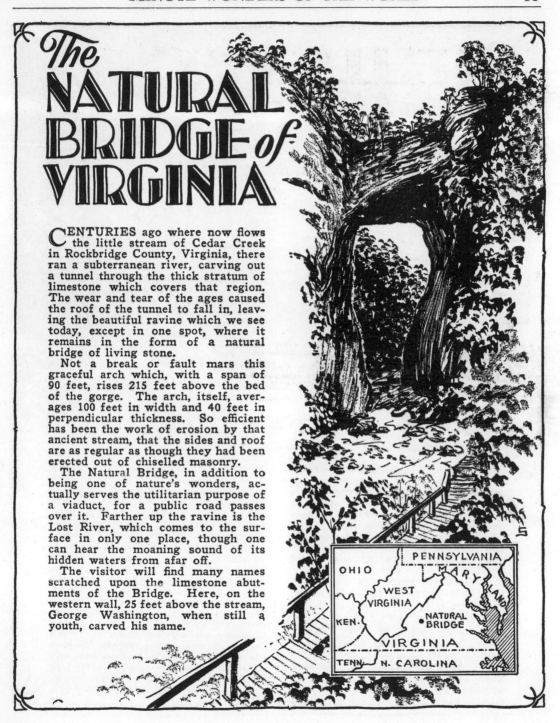

CENTURIES ago where now flows the little stream of Cedar Creek in Rockbridge County, Virginia, there ran a subterranean river, carving out a tunnel through the thick stratum of limestone which covers that region. The wear and tear of the ages caused the roof of the tunnel to fall in, leaving the beautiful ravine which we see today, except in one spot, where it remains in the form of a natural bridge of living stone.

Not a break or fault mars this graceful arch which, with a span of 90 feet, rises 215 feet above the bed of the gorge. The arch, itself, averages 100 feet in width and 40 feet in perpendicular thickness. So efficient has been the work of erosion by that ancient stream, that the sides and roof are as regular as though they had been erected out of chiselled masonry.

The Natural Bridge, in addition to being one of nature's wonders, actually serves the utilitarian purpose of a viaduct, for a public road passes over it. Farther up the ravine is the Lost River, which comes to the surface in only one place, though one can hear the moaning sound of its hidden waters from afar off.

The visitor will find many names scratched upon the limestone abutments of the Bridge. Here, on the western wall, 25 feet above the stream, George Washington, when still a youth, carved his name.

The FALLS of the NIAGARA

Cave of the Winds and Rock of Ages.

ON AN average 1,000,000 people journey every year to view the grandeur and beauty of the Niagara cataract, which before the coming of the white men was known by the Indians as "thundering water," the dwelling place of the Great Spirit.

Millions of years ago the Falls, separated by Goat Island into the American and the Canadian, or Horseshoe Fall, now located about seventeen miles downriver from Buffalo, tumbled over the steep escarpment at Lewiston and Queenston, seven miles still farther down the river. As they wore away the limestone cliff, at an average rate of five feet a year, they dug the great gorge through which the turbulent waters of the Great Lakes dash today.

The American Fall is 162 feet high, but only 1400 feet broad, while the Horseshoe Fall, with a curving crest of 2600 feet, is 155 feet high. It is estimated that an average of 200,000 cubic feet of water plunge over the Falls every second. This volume was greater in the days before the power companies began utilizing the water for electric power. Beneath the layer of limestone the rushing cataract has hollowed out of the softer shale the famous "Cave of the Winds," and at the foot of the Falls a deep pool has been scooped out into which the waters plunge with a mighty roar. The land surrounding both Falls is a public reservation.

"OLD FAITHFUL" GEYSER

THERE are other geysers in that land of wonders, Yellowstone National Park, which have more powerful eruptions—such as the "Giant," "Giantess," "Grand," "Splendid," and "Excelsior" geysers. The "Bee Hive" and the "Great Fountain" have more interesting formations, but it is to "Old Faithful," first discovered and first named, that every visitor pays his tribute.

Once every 60 to 63 minutes, almost as regular as the striking of a clock, there rises from a fissure in the twelve-foot-high mound of rock a 150-foot column of scalding water, estimated by scientists to be 1,500,000 gallons each eruption—more than 33,-000,000 gallons per day. That's almost enough to supply the hot baths and radiators of a city of 300,000 people!

The word geyser comes from the Icelandic *geysir*, which means gusher. The geyser tube (in the case of "Old Faithful," it measures from two to six feet in diameter), usually formed by a rock fissure whose sides have been lined by silica deposits, leads down into the interior of the earth, where the water at the base of the tube comes into contact with molten rock and is turned into steam. As the pressure of the steam reaches a certain head, the whole column of water is shot into the air. This process is repeated with clocklike regularity.

Geyser fields are also found in Iceland, New Zealand, the Malay Archipelago, and South America.

MONTANA

YELLOWSTONE NATIONAL PARK

GRAND CANYON

IDAHO

WYOMING

YELLOWSTONE LAKE

OLD FAITHFUL GEYSER

C ----- STEAM POCKET
A - B --- WATER LEVEL
E

A   C   B
      D

BOILING WATER ------D
CREATES STEAM -----C
CAUSING ERUPTIONS---E

The PALISADES of the HUDSON

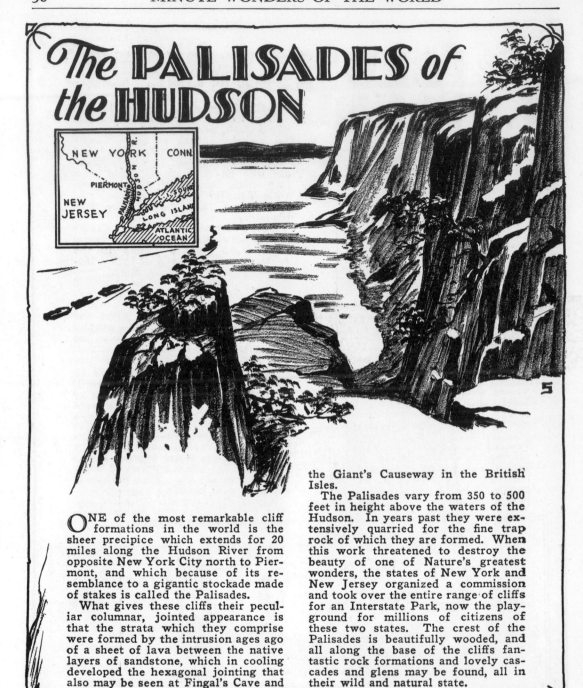

ONE of the most remarkable cliff formations in the world is the sheer precipice which extends for 20 miles along the Hudson River from opposite New York City north to Piermont, and which because of its resemblance to a gigantic stockade made of stakes is called the Palisades.

What gives these cliffs their peculiar columnar, jointed appearance is that the strata which they comprise were formed by the intrusion ages ago of a sheet of lava between the native layers of sandstone, which in cooling developed the hexagonal jointing that also may be seen at Fingal's Cave and the Giant's Causeway in the British Isles.

The Palisades vary from 350 to 500 feet in height above the waters of the Hudson. In years past they were extensively quarried for the fine trap rock of which they are formed. When this work threatened to destroy the beauty of one of Nature's greatest wonders, the states of New York and New Jersey organized a commission and took over the entire range of cliffs for an Interstate Park, now the playground for millions of citizens of these two states. The crest of the Palisades is beautifully wooded, and all along the base of the cliffs fantastic rock formations and lovely cascades and glens may be found, all in their wild and natural state.

The PANAMA CANAL

Coming through Culebra Cut.

FOR four centuries men had been trying to find a way to sail through the Isthmus of Panama and save the tedious trip around South America. Columbus tried; in 1529 Charles V of Spain ordered a vain survey; from 1825 on there were various futile American schemes.

In 1876 De Lesseps, engineer of the Suez Canal, headed a French company, in which thousands of families invested their savings, to build a sea-level canal. The French laborers found living in the tropic heat and the dense insect-filled forests a constant torture, and died so rapidly that Panama was called "The White Man's Graveyard." After seven years the plan failed, ending in a scandal.

In 1903 the United States finally bought the Panama works and the present lock system was evolved by General Goethals. Living conditions were made possible by cleaning up the Isthmus, improving drainage and sewage, and fighting mosquitoes.

Even then the difficulties were almost unsurmountable. Great dams to protect the ocean mouths had to be constructed in shifting silt and ooze. The Culebra Cut had to be carved through the mountain backbone, and there were endless landslides.

Finally, due to three marvelous sets of locks, twelve in all, the stupendous project was successfully achieved; and now this 50-mile passageway, an engineering miracle, saves 8000 miles for a vessel voyaging from coast to coast.

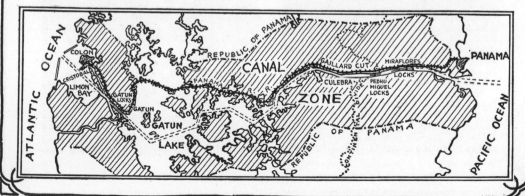

Natural Bridge

The PETRIFIED FOREST of ARIZONA

IN APACHE COUNTY, Arizona, is an area of some ten square miles, containing the Petrified Forest, which has kept geologists guessing ever since it was first discovered. Here, scattered about the ground, are found the fossilized remains of innumerable tree trunks, some in short sections, like stone cartwheels, others like the Petrified Bridge, which stretches, a great stone "log," 111 feet long and 10 feet in circumference, across a small canyon, forming a bridge over which one may ride horseback.

Millions of years ago, according to scientists, this tree and the others whose petrified remains now lie exposed probably grew to a height of from 175 to 200 feet in a forest thousands of miles distant! Back in those dim times, when the young world was subject to greater convulsions of nature than it is today, a great flood uprooted those ancient trees and bore them far away. Through the years they disintegrated, and as the wood fiber decayed, the lime and iron and other minerals held in solution in the water took their place, until what was once a log of wood became a "log" of solid stone.

Then came other volcanic disturbances, lowering and again lifting the region where the tree trunks had lodged. Erosion by wind and atmosphere wore away the softer rock, leaving exposed to the light of our times the fossil trunks of a forest of trees which raised their stalwart trunks into the skies many millions of years ago.

The snout of the Saskatchewan Glacier, showing crevasse on right

RIVERS of ICE (Glaciers)

GLACIERS, those slow-moving rivers of ice formed by snow masses creeping down from the regions of perennial frost to warmer altitudes below, naturally are more numerous in arctic and antarctic latitudes, but they are also to be found wherever there are mountains high enough to receive all their moisture in the form of snow. There are even glaciers directly on the equator among the higher peaks of the Andes, in Peru and Bolivia, where the snow line lies close to 17,500 feet.

The Alpine glaciers, the largest of which is the Aletsch, ten miles in length, perhaps are the best known, because they are so accessible to the traveler, but the glaciers of Alaska and British Columbia are the largest in the world. Of the 5000 known to exist between latitudes 56° and 60° on the Pacific coast, only a few have been named or mapped. Most of them have never been seen. Twenty-five of them discharge into the sea, great masses of ice breaking off to become those menaces to navigation, icebergs.

The rate of flow of the rivers of ice varies from 15 to 20 inches a year in the Alps to 21 to 90 feet a day in Greenland. From a distance they appear to be smooth and solid, but at close range one observes that they are broken transversely by deep crevasses, and that they are mottled with long, dark bands made up of boulders and rock débris called moraines, which they deposit where the ice melts.

The SEQUOIA FOREST of CALIFORNIA

ON THE western slope of the High Sierras in middle California grow the wonderful sequoia trees, a forest, more than 2000 years old, of giants 200 feet high and 30 feet in diameter.

A single trunk of one of these trees would block a modern highway; six automobiles could hide side by side behind one of these great boles; placed in a city street, their lowest branches would look into the thirteenth story of a skyscraper; their size dwarfs everything about them and baffles description.

Their extreme age is due to the fact that they are almost indestructible. There is no record of any sequoia dying from age or disease. Forest fires have swept through them many times, but the spongelike armor of reddish bark acts like asbestos protection. Insects cannot destroy them, for their drill holes fill with a tanninlike dust that chokes them. Cold and frost cannot penetrate the exterior. The soft, brittle interior wood seems never to rot, and any scar is soon coated over with a thick healing sap.

The most venerable tree is the General Sherman, estimated to be 4000 to 5000 years in age, and supposed to be the oldest living thing on earth. Its circumference is 102.7 feet at the base. It is a strange sensation to look up into the vast reaches of that veteran 175 feet high. It has seen dinosaurs about its feet in its youth, and was old when Cheops was planning the Pyramids. It transcends time.

The SINGING TOWER

IN 1923, when Edward W. Bok conceived the idea of creating what many people now call the "Taj Mahal of America," Iron Mountain, Florida, a sandy, barren hill near Mountain Lake, had only one claim to distinction—that it was the highest point (324 feet) above sea level in the state.

Six years later, when the "Singing Tower" was dedicated on February 1, 1929, that sandhill had been transformed into one of the loveliest parks in all the world, with groves of trees, shining lakes where flamingoes preen their wings, plantations of flowering shrubs—a wonderful bird sanctuary some 50 acres in extent. Construction on the magnificent campanile which had for its inspiration the tower at Malines, Belgium, was begun in January, 1927. The granite base, 51 feet in width, is constructed upon a web of concrete piles sunk 24 feet below the surface of the ground. Above this to a height of 205 feet soars the beautiful tower of pink Georgia marble and tan ocquina stone from Florida, changing its form by graceful lines at the height of 150 feet until it becomes octagonal. Its eight windows, each 35 feet high, are of Gothic lace pattern worked in faïence, and above them the crown is elaborately carved. The main portal to the tower is of hand-wrought golden bronze.

The "Singing Tower" gets its name from the fact that it houses one of the largest carillons in the world—61 bells.

The STATUE of LIBERTY

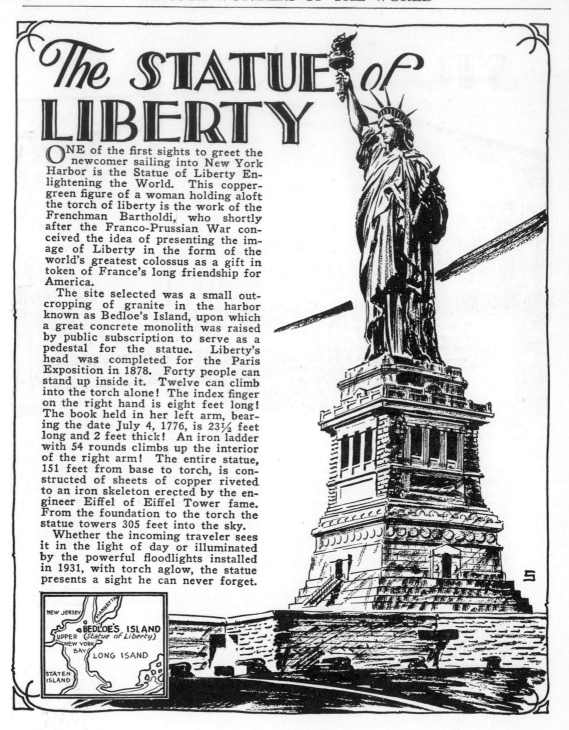

ONE of the first sights to greet the newcomer sailing into New York Harbor is the Statue of Liberty Enlightening the World. This copper-green figure of a woman holding aloft the torch of liberty is the work of the Frenchman Bartholdi, who shortly after the Franco-Prussian War conceived the idea of presenting the image of Liberty in the form of the world's greatest colossus as a gift in token of France's long friendship for America.

The site selected was a small outcropping of granite in the harbor known as Bedloe's Island, upon which a great concrete monolith was raised by public subscription to serve as a pedestal for the statue. Liberty's head was completed for the Paris Exposition in 1878. Forty people can stand up inside it. Twelve can climb into the torch alone! The index finger on the right hand is eight feet long! The book held in her left arm, bearing the date July 4, 1776, is 23½ feet long and 2 feet thick! An iron ladder with 54 rounds climbs up the interior of the right arm! The entire statue, 151 feet from base to torch, is constructed of sheets of copper riveted to an iron skeleton erected by the engineer Eiffel of Eiffel Tower fame. From the foundation to the torch the statue towers 305 feet into the sky.

Whether the incoming traveler sees it in the light of day or illuminated by the powerful floodlights installed in 1931, with torch aglow, the statue presents a sight he can never forget.

NEW JERSEY — MANHATTAN

BEDLOE'S ISLAND
(Statue of Liberty)

UPPER NEW YORK BAY — LONG ISAND

STATEN ISLAND

STONE MOUNTAIN

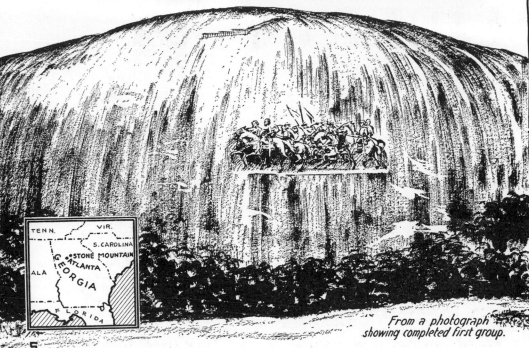

From a photograph showing completed first group.

A FEW miles northeast of the city of Atlanta, in De Kalb County, Georgia, a dome-shaped hill of granite rises over 800 feet above the surrounding plain. Grim and gray, with scarcely a sign of vegetation, except where a few shrubs have taken root in crannies in the naked rock, Stone Mountain has stood, a stern sentinel, since the beginning of time. The northern face of the mountain presents an almost vertical cliff 300 feet high and worn smooth by the elements.

In 1916 Gutzon Borglum, the sculptor, a pupil of Rodin's, conceived the idea of carving in relief upon this northern slope a gigantic memorial to the lost cause of the Confederacy. The design, as he planned it, was to dwarf even the colossal Ramessean figures of Abu Simbel, hewn in the rock cliffs along the Nile. Two hundred feet in height and 1300 feet long, the carving was to represent the Confederate army on the march, with Robert E. Lee and his generals at its head.

Borglum began work in 1917, but the war intervened. When it was taken up again in 1923, a dispute arose, Borglum was dismissed, and the work placed in charge of Augustus Lukeman. The head of Lee was unveiled in 1924, but only a part of the gigantic army of living stone has as yet been completed because of lack of funds. The pageant eventually will comprise 52 mounted figures, and below them a Memorial Hall to be cut out of the solid rock.

"THE BORE" — INCOMING TIDE OF THE BAY OF FUNDY

Bear River at low tide — When the tide comes up it completely fills the river bed. A typical view

TIDES in the BAY of FUNDY

IN LONGFELLOW'S poem "Evangeline" he speaks of the Acadians along the Basin of Minas building dikes to "shut out the turbulent tides."

It is in the Basin of Minas and Chignecto Bay, two arms of the Bay of Fundy, extending between Nova Scotia and New Brunswick, where occur those phenomenal tides of 50 to 60 feet, the greatest tidal range of any place on earth.

Tides, as everyone knows, are those periodic risings and fallings of the sea level due to the attraction of the moon and sun as the earth rotates upon its axis, causing the piling up and flattening out of the waters into high and low tides. Two high waters and two low waters occur each 24 hours. Twice each month, at new moon and full moon, when the sun and moon are pulling together, a larger tidal range known as spring tide results. Neap tides, with smaller ranges, occur when the moon is in its first and last quarters.

Possibly because of the influence of the Gulf Stream the tidal changes in the Bay of Fundy are particularly violent. At low tide one sees vast expanses of mud flats, and the inreaching estuaries are completely drained. In the case of one of these, the Petitcodiac River, where the advancing tide is concentrated on a steadily narrowing front which the river cannot accommodate, a wave from four to six feet high is produced, known as a *bore*, which rushes upstream in the shape of a foaming wall of water.

INDIAN TOTEM POLES

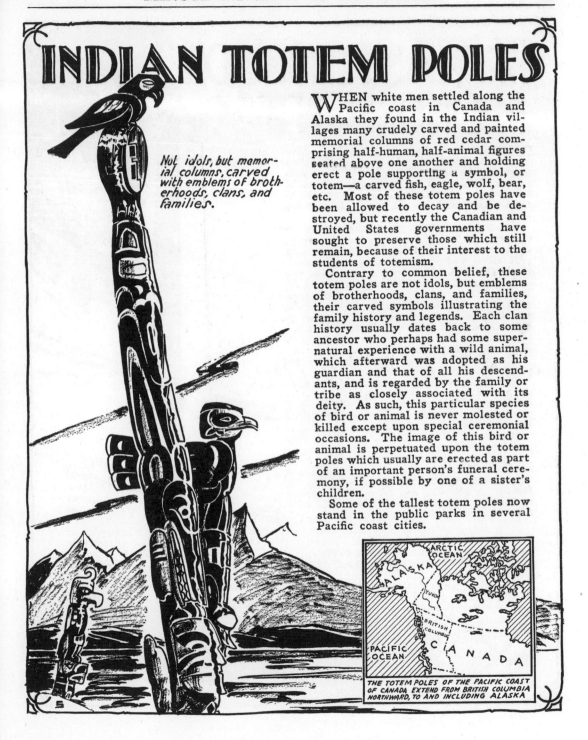

Not idols, but memorial columns, carved with emblems of brotherhoods, clans, and families.

WHEN white men settled along the Pacific coast in Canada and Alaska they found in the Indian villages many crudely carved and painted memorial columns of red cedar comprising half-human, half-animal figures seated above one another and holding erect a pole supporting a symbol, or totem—a carved fish, eagle, wolf, bear, etc. Most of these totem poles have been allowed to decay and be destroyed, but recently the Canadian and United States governments have sought to preserve those which still remain, because of their interest to the students of totemism.

Contrary to common belief, these totem poles are not idols, but emblems of brotherhoods, clans, and families, their carved symbols illustrating the family history and legends. Each clan history usually dates back to some ancestor who perhaps had some supernatural experience with a wild animal, which afterward was adopted as his guardian and that of all his descendants, and is regarded by the family or tribe as closely associated with its deity. As such, this particular species of bird or animal is never molested or killed except upon special ceremonial occasions. The image of this bird or animal is perpetuated upon the totem poles which usually are erected as part of an important person's funeral ceremony, if possible by one of a sister's children.

Some of the tallest totem poles now stand in the public parks in several Pacific coast cities.

THE TOTEM POLES OF THE PACIFIC COAST OF CANADA EXTEND FROM BRITISH COLUMBIA NORTHWARD, TO AND INCLUDING ALASKA

The WASHINGTON MONUMENT

THE austere shaft of gleaming white marble which may be seen from miles away as one approaches the city of Washington, D. C., well exemplifies the "dignity, symmetry, and towering height of Washington's character" in the minds of all his countrymen.

The popular movement to erect this giant obelisk, 555 feet high and 55 feet square at the base, began when the first President was still alive, and it is said that he, himself, chose the site. The foundations were not laid, however, until a half century later, in 1848, after a subscription fund had been started by Chief Justice Marshall. Work was suspended a few years later, when a block of marble from the Temple of Concord, Rome, sent by the Pope to be placed in the wall, disappeared, and the bitter controversy that followed caused the contributions to dwindle to nothing.

The shaft, one-third completed, was covered with a temporary roof, and there it stood, an unsightly stump, until the year of the Centennial, when public interest led to the completion of the memorial in 1884.

The walls of the obelisk are more than five feet thick at the base and three feet at the top, and are built of granite, faced with marble. They are said to contain a block of stone quarried from every state in the Union. A stairway and an elevator ascend to the top of the shaft, which is capped with a pyramid of gleaming aluminum.

② LINCOLN MEMORIAL   ③ CAPITOL

POTOMAC RIVER

TIDAL BASIN

① WASHINGTON MONUMENT

YELLOWSTONE NATIONAL PARK

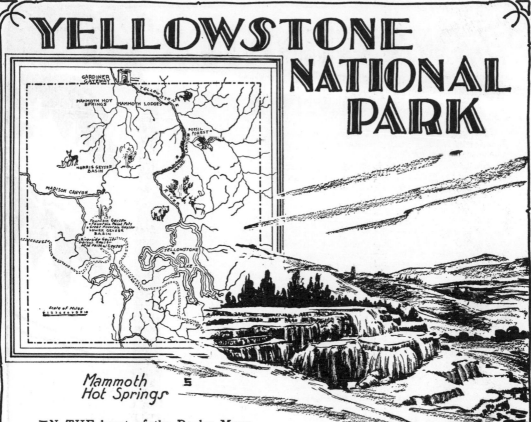

Mammoth Hot Springs

IN THE heart of the Rocky Mountains lies an area of 3350 square miles, most of it in the northwestern corner of Wyoming, which has been set aside by the nation as a public pleasure ground and called the Yellowstone National Park. The first recorded visit to this region was made by John Colter in 1810, when he took refuge there from hostile Indians. His stories of the marvels he found were wholly discredited for many years. And small wonder, for there is probably no region on earth of equal area which excels the Park in the variety and grandeur of its scenery.

Among the sights to delight the visitor, besides the 30 mountain peaks of 10,000 feet or more in altitude, is Yellowstone Lake, from which flows the Yellowstone River, whose waters plunge 417 feet over two noble cataracts into the Grand Canyon, where they dash between walls of fantastic colors 1200 to 1500 feet high.

Then there are the countless geysers and hot springs present everywhere—on mountain tops, in valleys—covering the ground with white incrustations of silica streaked with bright colors, and emitting sulphurous fumes. Among the more famous ones are the Mammoth Hot Springs, near the northern entrance to the park. These springs have built up terraces of basins several hundred feet high, each basin from one to eight feet in diameter, of beautifully colored silica. The water issues boiling at the summit and gradually cools as it reaches the lower basins.

The YOSEMITE FALLS

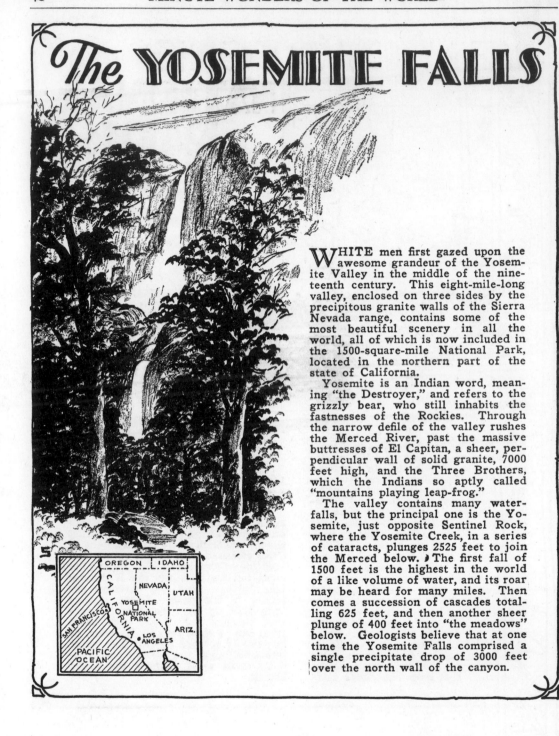

WHITE men first gazed upon the awesome grandeur of the Yosemite Valley in the middle of the nineteenth century. This eight-mile-long valley, enclosed on three sides by the precipitous granite walls of the Sierra Nevada range, contains some of the most beautiful scenery in all the world, all of which is now included in the 1500-square-mile National Park, located in the northern part of the state of California.

Yosemite is an Indian word, meaning "the Destroyer," and refers to the grizzly bear, who still inhabits the fastnesses of the Rockies. Through the narrow defile of the valley rushes the Merced River, past the massive buttresses of El Capitan, a sheer, perpendicular wall of solid granite, 7000 feet high, and the Three Brothers, which the Indians so aptly called "mountains playing leap-frog."

The valley contains many waterfalls, but the principal one is the Yosemite, just opposite Sentinel Rock, where the Yosemite Creek, in a series of cataracts, plunges 2525 feet to join the Merced below. The first fall of 1500 feet is the highest in the world of a like volume of water, and its roar may be heard for many miles. Then comes a succession of cascades totalling 625 feet, and then another sheer plunge of 400 feet into "the meadows" below. Geologists believe that at one time the Yosemite Falls comprised a single precipitate drop of 3000 feet over the north wall of the canyon.

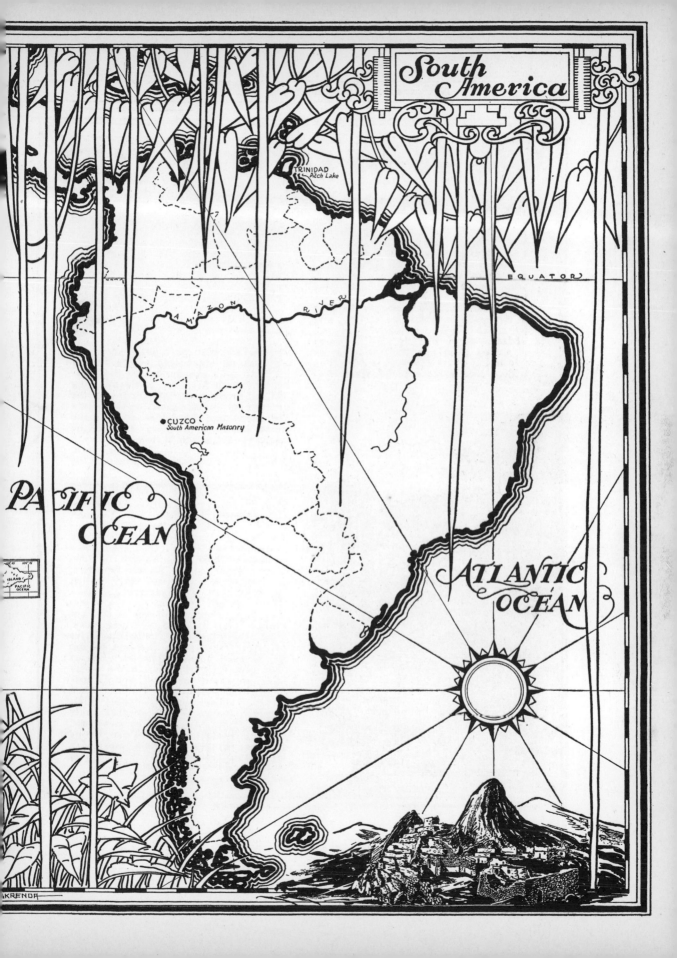

South America

TRINIDAD
Pitch Lake

EQUATOR

AMAZON RIVER

●CUZCO
South American Masonry

PACIFIC
OCEAN

ISLAND
PACIFIC
OCEAN

ATLANTIC
OCEAN

AKRENDA

The AMAZON RIVER

WHEN the Spanish explorer Orellana in the year 1541 deserted his commander Pizarro and followed the giant river, the largest in all the world, which flows 3300 miles from the Peruvian Andes to the sea, he named it the Amazon, in honor of the women of some of the native tribes who fought side by side with their husbands.

For 2300 miles the mighty Amazon is navigable to ocean steamships, and 500 miles still farther inland to vessels of lesser draft. For most of its course it varies from one to two miles in width, but at its mouth it is 160 miles wide. Every second the river discharges 5,000,000 cubic feet of water far out into the Atlantic.

Over most of the 2½ millions of square miles of area it drains (a territory equal in extent to about 85 per cent of that of the United States) the rainfall amounts to over 100 inches a year. As a result, dense tropical vegetation lines its entire course and its 20 principal tributaries.

After the Amazon enters Brazil, its elevation is only 300 feet above sea level, and its waters become very deep and sluggish. The ocean tide's influence is felt up the river for a distance of 400 miles. Despite the millions of tons of silt which it annually brings down to the sea, it finds difficult work to build itself a delta, because of the constant warfare with the ocean and its fierce tidal bores which eat away the coast faster than the river silt can build it up.

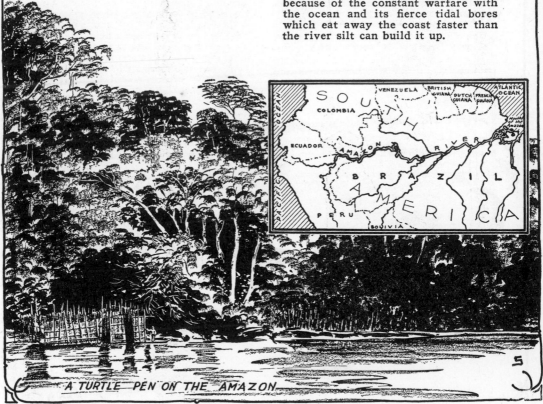

A TURTLE PEN ON THE AMAZON

The IMAGES of EASTER ISLAND

ON EASTER DAY in 1722 the Dutch Admiral Roggeveen, cruising the open Pacific 2000 miles west of South America, came upon a tiny, desolate island whose coast was thronged with a weird crowd of stone images. These showed giants from the waist up, 6 to 30 feet high, with crude flat heads and ears with strangely distended lobes. A few, evidently important, wore round hats or crowns of a different red stone. Many had toppled from the long paved platforms where they had originally stood. Several were scrolled with mysterious symbols.

These statues have defied explanation through the years. The island is only thirteen by seven miles. The 250 natives who eke out a miserable existence there know nothing of their origin or purpose. Yet explorers have found 150 half-cut statues lying in the quarries on the side of an extinct volcano, while over 300 finished specimens have been found placed in different parts of the island.

The most sacred spot was the burial ground near the coast, where the crowned giants stood on "ahu," massive platforms of masonry, evidently to guard the bodies laid out till their bones were buried. This was approached from inland by a long aisle guarded by a double row of statues.

The carving, moving, and raising of these giants must have been the labor of centuries; yet the only trace of the unknown makers is the primitive stone tools scattered near the quarry, where the work was evidently abandoned suddenly, no one knows why or when.

PERSPECTIVE MODEL

VAULTS

BACK FACES SEA

DIAGRAM OF AN IMAGE AHU

EASTER ISLAND

PACIFIC OCEAN

The PITCH LAKE of TRINIDAD

SIX miles off the coast of Venezuela lies the island of Trinidad, which was discovered by Columbus in the year 1496. As part of the Spanish Main it has had a colorful history. In the days before Sir Walter Raleigh sacked and burned its capital, San José de Oruna, galleons laden with gold would sail forth from its harbors. Today most of the ships are loaded with a black, evil-smelling substance called asphalt, much in demand in the cities of North America.

For on the island of Trinidad is located the famous Pitch Lake, a circular pit only 104 acres in area and three miles in circumference, but from which comes an almost inexhaustible supply of asphalt, used for street pavements. Pressure from below forces the pitch up in great bubbles which harden sufficiently around the edges to bear one's weight, but in the center remain in a liquid state. Some of the congealed forma-tions are like huge mushrooms, separated by fissures where the rainwater collects into pools. Millions of tons of asphalt have been dug from the lake, but no impression seems to have been made upon its contents.

The pitch has impregnated the soil for miles around the lake. The road which leads to La Brea is actually built upon a bed of asphalt, and, like a glacier, it is slowly moving toward the sea.

ON THE "BOTTOMLESS" ASPHALT LAKE

ATLANTIC OCEAN
TRINIDAD
VENEZUELA
SOUTH AMERICA

SOUTH AMERICAN MASONRY

THE remarkable stone relics found in South America have been roughly classed as Inca ruins. However, the Incas were a comparatively late civilization—about 1100 A.D.—and their masonry was built upon a foundation antedating them many centuries.

The two types are similar—massive, severe, sombre, like the mountains about them; but the earlier masonry was much more complicated, for there stones of many angles were fitted together, while the Incas used the simpler rectangular construction. There are primitive walls in Cuzco, afterwards the Inca capital, where stones of as many as twelve sides were used, each stone, of course, being laboriously fitted to just one place, and the walls have stood for ages without mortar or cement. Some of these stones weighed twenty tons apiece and were hewn out with only the crudest stone chisels. The result looks like the work of patient, plodding giants.

There was practically no decoration in either masonry, though the Incas placed oblong niches at intervals to vary their wall spaces, and occasionally their predecessors did some rugged carving over doorways.

So through Ecuador, Peru, Bolivia, and part of Chile one sees these stern reminders of peoples who lived a hard existence, perching their towns in mountain fastnesses and guarding the narrow approaches with forbidding walls and fortresses which then defied enemies and have since defied time.

PROPYLEA

ERECTHEUM

PARTHENON

PLAN OF THE ACROPOLIS ~

The ACROPOLIS, Athens

"ACROPOLIS" was the ancient name for any citadel, but because of the long supremacy of Athens, and because of her outstanding magnificence, her fortified hill and its renowned group of buildings are called "The Acropolis."

Admirably fitted by nature to withstand sieges because of its great height and the springs at its base, this rocky summit was used as a citadel as far back as the days of the Stone Age.

Originally it was surrounded by a double wall enclosing huts and market stalls on the plain, and temples and altars on the hill.

The Persians completely demolished these first buildings, but their destruction merely served to free the noble site for the geniuses of the Greek classical period, who under Themis-tocles, Cimon, and Pericles during the fifth century B.C. restored the walls and defenses and built that amazing group of majestic temples, the Parthenon, the Erechtheum, the Propylæa, the Temple of Nike, Victory, and many others.

These beautifully designed and perfectly proportioned shrines lifted their colonnades of gleaming marble and colored friezes of Greek history against the blue Athens sky in unforgettable grandeur. The giant statue of Athene, the patron goddess, was so set that the gleam of her helmet and spear could be seen far out at sea by mariners approaching the city.

Invasions, pillage, earthquakes—every possible vicissitude has shattered and marred the Acropolis, but its mutilated remains still have an impressive and inextinguishable majesty.

The ALHAMBRA

A FORTIFIED wall flanked with towers surrounds 35 acres of parks on a terrace plateau in Granada. Here through avenues of trees—roses, oranges, and myrtles planted by the Moors, and elms brought in 1812 by Wellington—one approaches the mysterious stronghold-palace which Al Ahmar and his successors built from 1248 to 1354. This ornate Moorish masterpiece is a combination citadel and palace, with residences for courtiers, and subterranean cells, called the Martyr's Villa, where the Christian labor-slaves were confined.

In spite of centuries of depredations and vandalism and inappropriate alterations by many rulers, the Alhambra's intrinsic Moorish quality remains. Its myriad columned and arched courts are marvels of intricate lacy, colored stonework, with vaulted ceilings twisting with arabesques and dripping stalactites of delicately shaped stucco. The windows are latticed and trellised, and every inch of the embroidered walls is mosaicked with Arabic mottoes interlaced with garlands and festoons. Many of the courts contain carved fountains and pools wherein the infinite traceries of walls and ceilings are reflected.

In spite of the beauty, however, one cannot forget the stern and bloody history of this castle, especially in the Great Hall, where Boabdil, last king of Granada, invited a company of his chiefs to a banquet and then massacred them.

Towers Princess, Alhambra

The APPIAN WAY

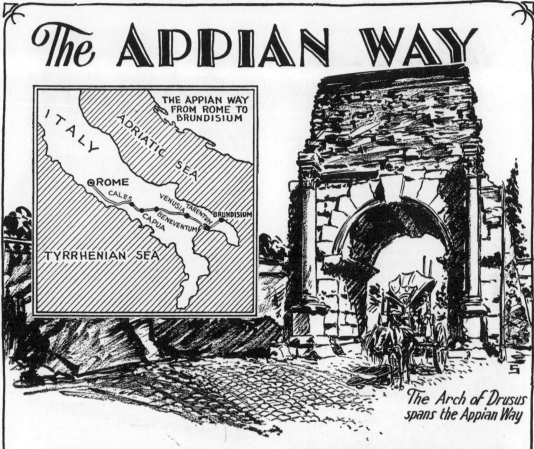

THE APPIAN WAY FROM ROME TO BRUNDISIUM

ITALY
ADRIATIC SEA
ROME
CALES
VENUSIA TARENTUM
BRUNDISIUM
BENEVENTUM
CAPUA
TYRRHENIAN SEA

The Arch of Drusus spans the Appian Way

IN THE year 312 B.C. Appius Claudius Cæcus, then Roman censor, began the construction of the famous highway which, even now, after 22 centuries, is still partially in use. The poet Statius well named this road, which connected the capital city with all Southern Italy, Regina Viarum ("the queen of roads").

The road, built on a carefully laid foundation of cemented rocks, was paved with large hexagonal blocks of basaltic lava, beautifully fitted together. Originally it ran only as far as Capua, a distance of 132 miles, but as more and more of the peninsula was conquered, it was extended to Beneventum, Venusia, Tarentum, and Brundisium—366 miles over mountain, marsh, and plain from Rome. Horace writes of riding muleback over this road as far as Beneventum.

For the first few miles out of the city (it led from the Porta Capena in the Servian Wall) the highway was lined with tombs, among them those of the Scipios. For many leagues it stretched southward as straight as a plummet line, even over the steep grades of the Alban Hills and over the Pontine Marshes. Well-preserved bridges still attest the skill and resourcefulness of the engineers in charge of the work. Stone mileposts remain to trace the route where the roadway itself has disappeared.

Later rulers, Trajan, Hadrian, Diocletian, and even Theodoric, as late as 486 A.D., repaired and extended this most famous of all the Roman roads.

The STRANGE FORTS of ARAN

THE strange tumbled stone forts of Aran stand on the stormy coasts of the three Aran Islands off Galway, once the outer rim of the known world. These islands, according to legend, were inhabited by a race of giants and magic workers. Probably they were settled by adventurous sea pirates who chose that fierce, lonely outpost as a headquarters, building the forts in the Bronze Age, 1800 to 400 B.C.

Not a tree grows on these wind-swept, rocky islands, whose precipitous gray cliffs rise abruptly from the Atlantic. The masonry of the old forts is piled on top of the limestone cliffs. The largest fort is Dun Aengusa (Fort of Aengus), probably the walled citadel of the ruler. Covering sixteen acres, it could have sheltered 3000 people in case of attack. However, a siege was not expected, for it contained no well or spring of water. There were two rings of walls, one seven and one thirteen feet thick, and often eighteen feet high. The huts and galleries and booths which were once enclosed there were probably wooden, for they have all disappeared.

Ireland was then of great importance because of its gold and copper. Warlike tribes roamed the land, pillaging and plundering. Tradition says they were finally driven off to the Aran Islands, where the fugitive chieftains fortified themselves for another 200 years of piracy and raiding. What finally dispersed them is as mysterious as the forts they have left.

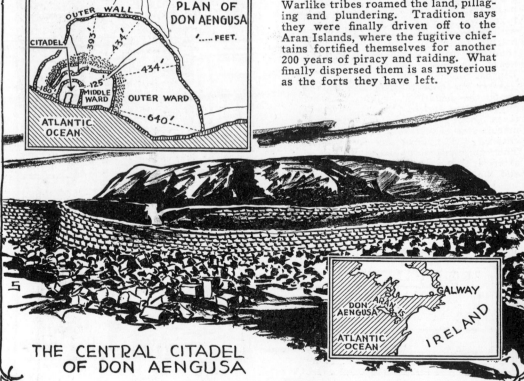

PLAN OF DON AENGUSA
'....FEET.
OUTER WALL
CITADEL
393'
434'
434'
180'
125'
MIDDLE WARD
OUTER WARD
640'
ATLANTIC OCEAN

GALWAY
DON AENGUSA
ARAN
ATLANTIC OCEAN
IRELAND

THE CENTRAL CITADEL OF DON AENGUSA

The BATHS of DIOCLETIAN

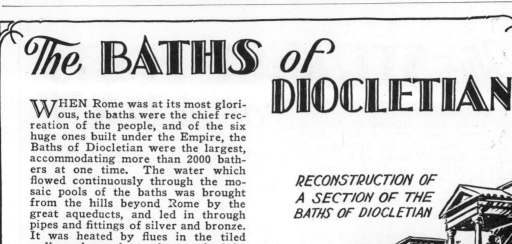

WHEN Rome was at its most glorious, the baths were the chief recreation of the people, and of the six huge ones built under the Empire, the Baths of Diocletian were the largest, accommodating more than 2000 bathers at one time. The water which flowed continuously through the mosaic pools of the baths was brought from the hills beyond Rome by the great aqueducts, and led in through pipes and fittings of silver and bronze. It was heated by flues in the tiled walls, and one chose whatever bath he preferred, cold, tepid, warm, shower, or perspiration.

The crowds came on foot or in litters prepared to spend the day, for these vast baths, as large as a town, provided a wide range of entertainment and were like great clubs. The foyer was a brilliantly painted hall with lofty ceiling upheld by colored marble columns. Here by playing fountains one greeted acquaintances, heard the news, and read the Acta Diurna, the newspaper.

After the chosen bath, one walked about the beautiful grounds, amidst clipped yew and box hedges, cypress trees, gorgeous flowers, and gleaming marble statues. If very energetic, one entered the gymnasium for sports. Then followed a luxurious meal, and afterwards the libraries, concert halls, and theatre rooms provided diversion.

RECONSTRUCTION OF
A SECTION OF THE
BATHS OF DIOCLETIAN

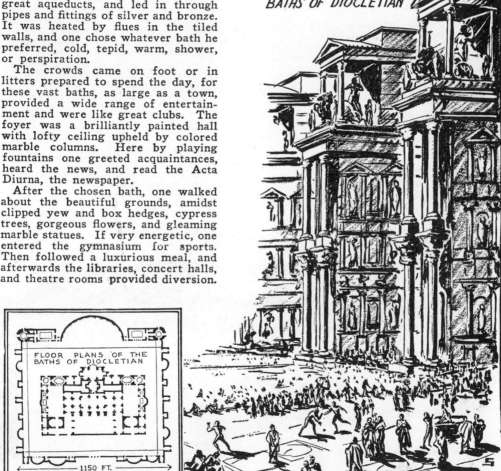

FLOOR PLANS OF THE BATHS OF DIOCLETIAN

←——— 1150 FT. ———→

The GREAT BELL of MOSCOW

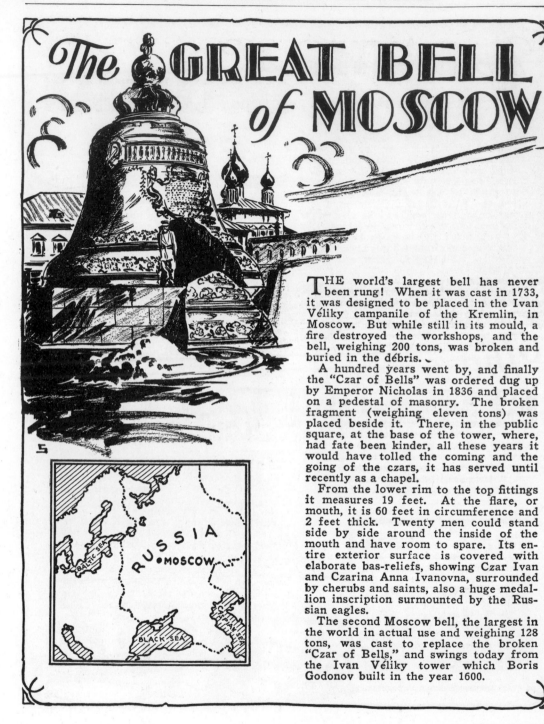

THE world's largest bell has never been rung! When it was cast in 1733, it was designed to be placed in the Ivan Véliky campanile of the Kremlin, in Moscow. But while still in its mould, a fire destroyed the workshops, and the bell, weighing 200 tons, was broken and buried in the débris.

A hundred years went by, and finally the "Czar of Bells" was ordered dug up by Emperor Nicholas in 1836 and placed on a pedestal of masonry. The broken fragment (weighing eleven tons) was placed beside it. There, in the public square, at the base of the tower, where, had fate been kinder, all these years it would have tolled the coming and the going of the czars, it has served until recently as a chapel.

From the lower rim to the top fittings it measures 19 feet. At the flare, or mouth, it is 60 feet in circumference and 2 feet thick. Twenty men could stand side by side around the inside of the mouth and have room to spare. Its entire exterior surface is covered with elaborate bas-reliefs, showing Czar Ivan and Czarina Anna Ivanovna, surrounded by cherubs and saints, also a huge medallion inscription surmounted by the Russian eagles.

The second Moscow bell, the largest in the world in actual use and weighing 128 tons, was cast to replace the broken "Czar of Bells," and swings today from the Ivan Véliky tower which Boris Godonov built in the year 1600.

The BLUE GROTTO, CAPRI

ONE of the strange things about the famous Blue Grotto on the island of Capri, only 20 miles away from the city of Naples, Italy, is that it was known to the people of ancient Rome, and then lost, not to be rediscovered until the early nineteenth century. Yet it is easy to understand why it should have become lost, for the mouth of this enchanted cave, which has been the despair of every artist who has ever visited it, is scarcely three feet high.

Like the many caves to be found on the island, the Blue Grotto has been carved out by the Mediterranean from the strata of Apennine limestone. Once you have entered it (and it can be done only when the sea is smooth), you are in a blue fairyland. Blues of every delicate tint and shade, from that of the sky to lapis lazuli, melt and mingle into one another, as a result of the refraction of the light which filters under the water through the small cavern mouth, and tinge the dim space of the grotto with the magic blue of the Bay of Naples.

The movement of the waves causes this light to be in a constant state of motion, like the movement on the screen of a huge color organ. The island of Capri also contains a Green Grotto and a White Grotto, which are well worth a visit, though they cannot equal the shimmering, opalescent beauty of the Blue Grotto.

CARCASSONNE

THE most perfect example in existence today of a mediæval walled fortress town is the Cité, or old town of Carcassonne, situated high above the banks of the river Aude in the south of France. The site is an ancient one, for there was a town here when Cæsar invaded Gaul. But the old town on the hill, as we now see it, with its double line of ramparts extending for nearly a mile, its 50 round towers and turrets, and massive citadel, for all the world like those of our best-loved fairy tales, dates back to the eleventh and twelfth centuries.

The "new town," as the inhabitants know it, dates from the thirteenth century, when the "old cité" rose in rebellion, and its expelled citizens founded a settlement on the opposite bank of the river.

It would require a whole book to relate the glamorous history of old Carcassonne, how it passed successively from the hands of Rome to the Visigoths, to the Arabs, to Pippen the Short, and finally to the Counts of Carcassonne, who ruled it independently until Simon de Montfort brought his Crusaders to its gates and forced Count Raymond Roger to yield; how in 1356 the citadel successfully resisted the Black Prince; how it finally was annexed to France in 1659.

The castle, which every tourist goes to see, belongs definitely to the eleventh and twelfth centuries, but the outer rampart was the work of Louis IX a full century later.

The ROMAN CATACOMBS

CENTURIES of persecution destroyed the first churches of the early Christians, but we still have one monument of their faith—the Catacombs. These mazes of underground galleries were dug out of tufa, volcanic rock, outside of Rome, where no burials were permitted. There are approximately 587 miles of them, containing 6,000,000 tombs.

But the Catacombs were more than cemeteries; they were the very cradle of Christianity, for it was in these secret subterranean vaults that the hunted groups of the devout gathered to sing hymns and pray and celebrate last rites, far from the garish Rome of voluptuous baths and gory amphitheatres. The halls were low and dark, with occasional dim light from airshafts; the shelves for the bodies lin-ing both sides, each grave walled with slabs of marble or baked clay with Biblical scenes and the name of the departed. At intervals the halls converged into small rooms where flaring tapers lighted the Christian services.

Yet contrary to expectation, these miles of tombs are not gruesome or horrible, but rather serene and beautiful, for the constant note of the decorations is peaceful and cheering. "Spes"—hope—is the word most frequently found in the brightly colored inscriptions. The most popular scenes are ones of deliverance, the Raising of Lazarus, Daniel in the Lions' Den, Peter's Escape from Prison, and everywhere in the shadowy underground light, the power and finality of death are denied.

The CIRCUS MAXIMUS

EVERY Roman town had its *circus*, which is the Latin name for an amphitheatre where horse and chariot races were held. The shape was usually that of an ellipse, down the center of which, lengthways, ran a wall, called the *spina*. It was around this wall that the races were run. The sides were arranged into tiers of seats, known as the *cavea*, with gangways and flights of steps for the convenience of the spectators.

At one end of the enclosure were the *carceres*, or stalls, twelve in number, arranged in a curve so as to be equidistant from the starting line. Above these stalls was the starter's box. On the *spina* were arranged three balls, or *ova*, resting on supports. As the chariots completed a lap, one of the balls was taken down, so the spectators knew how much of the race remained to be run.

The chief *circus* of Rome was the *Circus Maximus*, originally 1875 feet long, 625 feet wide, and over 312 feet high. As rebuilt by Cæsar, it accommodated 150,000 spectators, but was continually being enlarged, until in the fourth century it was said to be capable of seating 385,000 spectators! As Rome degenerated, the *circus* grew in popularity, and the rulers were continually being put to it to answer the cry of the debauched populace for *Panem et circenses*, which meant, "plenty to eat and free shows!" A wonderful description of a chariot race may be found in General Lew Wallace's novel, *Ben Hur*.

RECONSTRUCTION

The CLAUDIA AQUEDUCT

REMNANT OF THE
CLAUDIA AQUEDUCT

THE Claudia Aqueduct was built in 38 A.D., yet its huge arches, some of them broken, may still be seen stretching across the Campagna, and Rome today uses water from the conduits of which they once formed part.

The Roman builders had plenty of travertine stone and brick materials at hand. Pipes, on the contrary, were expensive, for there was no steel, cast iron was difficult to work, bronze was costly, and lead was unsuitable. So they built their waterlines above ground on the beautifully arched supports of masonry which still remain as their most distinctive contribution to architecture.

The Claudia was constructed of stone, and on reaching Rome its water was mingled with that of other aqueducts and carried on standing arches to a central point. Nine aqueducts brought about 40,000,000 gallons of water into the city every day, an allowance of about 40 gallons for a person. This huge amount was due to the wasteful system of continuous flow and to the popularity of the baths, which used quantities of water, the Baths of Diocletian alone accommodating 2000 bathers at a time.

The poor people carried water home in jars from the public fountains. But the rich had lead pipe lines stamped with their names laid at their own expense into their homes.

The great city could not have existed without the aqueducts, and those rugged arches still erect after centuries testify to the efficiency of Roman organization and engineering.

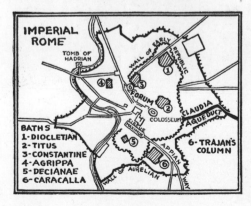

IMPERIAL ROME

TOMB OF HADRIAN

WALL OF EARLY REPUBLIC

FORUM

COLOSSEUM

CLAUDIA AQUEDUCT

APPIAN WAY

WALL OF AURELIAN

BATHS
1-DIOCLETIAN
2-TITUS
3-CONSTANTINE
4-AGRIPPA
5-DECIANAE
6-CARACALLA

6-TRAJAN'S COLUMN

The Cliff Monasteries of Meteora

AT THE northern side of the Peneius Valley in Northern Thessaly, thrust out from the main body of the Cambunian Mountains, are two great columnar masses of grayish brown rock, which have split away from their surroundings and stand apart like flat-topped towers. They are gaunt and precipitous, and it is amazing that anyone ever scaled their summits to rig up the rope and net worked by a windlass, and the flimsy ladder up the perpendicular face of the cliff, which now form the only means of ascent.

These bleak rock towers were chosen by Greek monks in the fourteenth century as a fitting place for monasteries which should be entirely separate from the evils of the world. Somehow they managed to huddle together 24 of them and maintain them for several centuries.

Now but four monasteries remain, and only about 30 persons still exist on that barren perch. Nevertheless, there is the chapel, the refectory, the cloisters, and numerous cells which were built under every possible difficulty. St. Stephen's, the richest of the convents, possesses one of the finest Byzantine chapels in Greece, while St. Barlaam's is famous for a rock-hewn chapel with beautiful antique frescoes.

The fourteenth century religious zeal, which conceived of such an isolated and difficult site for its monasteries is almost inconceivable to the twentieth century mind.

KALABAKA LIES AT THE FOOT OF THE PILLAR OF ROCKS OF METEORA

THE MAN MOTOR OF A THESSALIAN ELEVATOR

The COLOSSEUM of ROME

THE Colosseum, which the Romans knew as the Flavian amphitheatre, was begun by the Emperor Vespasian in 72 A.D. and completed by Domitian in 82 A.D., although a fourth story was added by Severus Alexander and Gordianus, 150 years later. It still remains as one of the most magnificent buildings in the world, though it has served as a quarry to supply building material for many of the largest structures in Rome. Its dimensions are gigantic. Built of white travertine, its vast oval measures 615 feet by 510 feet, and 157 feet in height. It was capable of seating 50,000 spectators, with standing room for 20,000 more.

In the days when Commodus used to go down into the arena to slay a few of his subjects for the amusement of the rest, a great awning covered the entire gigantic ellipse, supported by masts. One may still see the great sockets that held these masts in place. The seats were entirely of marble, but every slab of it has been stolen and used elsewhere.

Underneath the arena may still be seen the dens where the wild beasts, used in the combats, were kept, and the appliances for raising them to the level of the arena.

It is said that the Colosseum was opened with gladiatorial shows which lasted for a hundred days.

The CYCLOPEAN WALLS of TARRAGONA

ON A hill overlooking the Mediterranean, between Barcelona and Valencia, stands the old city of Tarragona, one-time capital of Roman Hispania, whose wealth came chiefly from the rare wines which it shipped to Rome. It is famous now because of the prehistoric walls, two miles long, which still surround the hill on three sides and which are so mysterious in origin and apparently superhuman in construction that they are known as the Cyclopean Walls.

In spite of the fact that during the Scipios and later under Cæsar Augustus, quantities of stone were rifled from these walls to use in city construction, they are still often 33 feet high. Fifty yoke of oxen could scarcely move some of the unhewn blocks of their foundations, yet there is no quarry anywhere near Tarragona. Whence came the stone to make those fortifications, standing for centuries in place without mortar or cement?

One gigantic gateway is in perfect condition. It is seven yards through, showing the thickness of the walls, one and one-half yards wide, two and one-half yards high, the jambs each formed of a single block, and the lintel reposing across them a solid stone measuring five yards.

One tower is sculptured with the strange face of a woman, full and round, with heavy lips and a flat nose. Probably mothers such as this one produced the giant race who reared the Cyclopean Walls of Tarragona.

The EIFFEL TOWER, Paris

ENGINEERS for years had longed to erect a tower 1000 feet high, but it was not until 1888 that the French engineer Eiffel worked out a practicable method. The Washington Monument had reached a height of 555 feet only with the greatest difficulty, because it was built of masonry. Eiffel's innovation was the use of iron for the framework.

It was raised on curved and braced pylons, similar to a viaduct, so that the superstructure could resist strong winds. Extensive excavations were made for a firm base, and four iron and masonry platforms sunk to hold the supports. These were felt to be absolutely level and firm, but in case of any settling which might throw the tower out of alignment, room was left on the foundations for hydraulic presses to insert steel wedges if necessary.

The weight of the framework alone is more than 7000 tons. Staircases and elevators connect the various floors of the tower. The first two platforms have covered galleries; and the third is a glass enclosed room 50 feet square, from which one may see 100 miles in all directions, or from which he may climb the winding stair to the light at the top.

The Eiffel tower is famous throughout the world as the outstanding landmark of Paris. It is constantly visited, and the fact that it can accommodate 5000 persons in a single hour gives some idea of its size.

The ESCURIAL

ANY Spaniard will tell you that the eighth wonder of the world is that grim combination of royal mausoleum, monastery, and church, frowning down from a height of 3432 feet above sea level in the mountains 30 miles northwest of Madrid.

It was Philip II, he who sent the Armada against England, who built this gigantic pantheon of Spain's monarchs, dedicating it, 23 years after the first stone was laid, to St. Laurence. And in memory of that Saint's martyrdom, he built the Escurial in the shape of a gridiron, 744 feet by 580 feet, covering an area of 400,000 square feet, surrounded by a high wall.

One has to view it from "Philip's Chair," a niche which the morbid monarch had cut into an overlooking mountain, from where he might daily watch the progress of his builders, to appreciate the immensity of this leaden gray pile, with its 12,000 windows and doors, its 95 miles of corridors, and its many Gothic towers surrounding the handsome Renaissance dome of its church.

Under the high altar of the church Philip had built a great octagonal crypt which was to serve as a mausoleum for the Spanish kings. Therein he installed the remains of the Emperor Charles V, leaving a vacant space beside his tomb, on which was inscribed in Spanish: "If any one of the descendants of Charles V excels him in the prowess of his deeds, let him occupy this niche; all others are reverently to abstain from encroaching." The niche is still vacant.

FINGAL'S CAVE

OFF the west coast of Scotland, on the North Channel, is the island of Staffa. Staffa is the Scandinavian equivalent of pillar, or staff, for its rock structure of columnar basalt is exactly that of the Giant's Causeway across the Channel on the Irish coast. The chief feature of the little island is the marvellous geological formation called Fingal's Cave.

Between two great columns of basalt 66 feet high and as perfectly shaped as though man had chiselled them, the sea has worn a cavern 42 feet wide and 227 feet long. The floor of this unique chamber with its pendent columns, of course, is the sea, and most beautiful are the color effects of the waves reflected upon the calcareous stalactites which form the roof. The sound of these waves, lapping against the walls of the cave, echoing and reverberating from the vaulted roof, is a hauntingly musical one,

which in time of storm becomes a thunderous roar. The cries of innumerable sea birds add to the endless clamor of the waves.

The discoverer of the cave is said to have been Sir Joseph Banks, who sailed with Captain Cook on one of his expeditions, and later, in 1772, in returning from a voyage to Iceland past the Hebrides and Staffa, visited the caves on the island. Wordsworth, Keats, Scott, Mendelssohn, and Tennyson have been among the visitors to Fingal's Cave.

The ROMAN FORUM

THE geographical center of ancient Rome was the Umbilicus, and about this succeeding emperors developed the Forum Romanum, the actual center of the life of the city and so of the whole world of that day. Originally this location had been marshy, as it lay between the Palatine and Capitoline Hills. But it was drained by the Cloaca Maxima, a great sewer built in 600 B.C. and still in use. The market stalls and places of barter were then removed to another section, for there was to be not one insignificant or unsightly building in this great plaza which represented the grandeur and prestige of Rome. Some of the most beautiful architecture of the ancient or modern world faced the Forum, which gleamed with white marble pillars, ornamented with gold and bronze, and abounded in sculptures, triumphal arches, and memorial columns.

The Temples of the Gods, the great prison, the huge Basilica Julia, the hall for civic and legal proceedings, the Senate house, the High Priest's house, the Public Tribunal, where any orator might express his views—all of these rose in grand and dignified proportions. At one end was the House of the Vestal Virgins, six maidens from the highest patrician families, pledged to remain unmarried for 30 years while they tended the Sacred Fire, or be buried alive.

The Sacred Way, oldest and most famous street, along which all processions passed, wound its way through the Forum up to the Capitol itself, which, from its hill, overlooked this living heart of Rome.

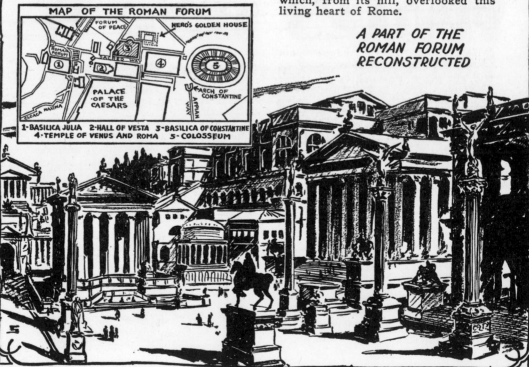

MAP OF THE ROMAN FORUM

FORUM OF PEACE

NERO'S GOLDEN HOUSE

ROMAN FORUM

SACRED WAY

PALACE OF THE CAESARS

ARCH OF CONSTANTINE

CLOACA MAXIMA

APPIAN WAY

1-BASILICA JULIA   2-HALL OF VESTA   3-BASILICA OF CONSTANTINE
4-TEMPLE OF VENUS AND ROMA   5-COLOSSEUM

A PART OF THE ROMAN FORUM RECONSTRUCTED

The GIANT'S CAUSEWAY

SURELY one of the unique spots of the globe is that bleak northern shore of the County Antrim, Ireland, where the Giant's Causeway leads down into the sea. And since it is Ireland, many legends have sprung up in explanation of these strange beds of gigantic, vertical, polygonal columns of solid basalt which stand as high as 200 feet above sea level.

One story is to the effect that the giant Fin Mac Coul built the great causeway across the sea to Scotland in order that his enemy, the Scottish giant, might be tempted to cross over to Ireland to his doom. To one standing upon the cliffs and looking down upon the uneven pavement of more than 40,000 closely-fitting hexagonal pillars (each one from 15 to 20 inches in diameter) it is easy to see how all those legends could originate. The amazing regularity of the columns makes them seem almost artificial.

The Giant's Causeway may be divided roughly into the Little, Middle, or Honeycomb, and the Grand Causeway. It is in the Middle Causeway where one may see the famous Wishing Chair, while on the Grand Causeway occur two strange formations called the Lady's Fan and the Giant's Loom, formed by a row of columns 30 feet high.

It is said that the despairing captain of one of the ships of the Spanish Armada fatally mistook the lofty stacks of Chimney Point for the chimneys of Dunlace Castle.

GIBRALTAR

MAP OF THE ROCK AND HARBOR FROM THE SPANISH LINES TO EUROPA POINT.

IN THE ancient days, when the Greeks and the Phoenicians sailed past what is now known as the Rock of Gibraltar, rising a sheer 1400 feet out of the waves of the Mediterranean, they called it and its companion promontory, Gebel Musa, on the African coast, the Pillars of Hercules. But the first people to recognize the strategic value of the rock were the Moors, who crossed the Straits in 711 A.D., building a castle upon it, and naming it "Gebel-el-Tarik," or the Mountain of Tarik, after their leader.

It was 900 years before Spain succeeded in getting rid of the Moors, and the last bit of ground they gave up when they left the Spanish peninsula was the Rock of Gibraltar. Charles V of Spain began the fortifications which now honeycomb the rock, their winding galleries hewn out of the living stone, but with the decline in the fortunes of Spain, the fortress fell into the hands of England. Napoleon tried in vain to take it away, for he recognized it as the key to the Mediterranean, and the battle of Trafalgar was fought not far away.

Thackeray calls it "the very image of an enormous lion, crouched between the Atlantic and the Mediterranean, and set there to guard the passage for its British mistress."

"Gib" is considered one of the few really impregnable fortresses of the world, and the secrets of its many galleries and masked portholes are jealously guarded by the British War Department.

The GIRALDA, SEVILLE

DURING the days when the Moors occupied the city of Seville, Spain, they built a beautiful mosque, with a minaret of stone and brick rising 250 feet above the street. That was far back about the end of the twelfth century. Then, as the Moslems were slowly evicted from the Spanish peninsula, the Christians made haste to tear down the infidel mosque and erected a church in its place. But the beautiful campanile was saved. A superstructure, or steeple, was added and topped by a weathervane, and the tower from which the muezzin used to call the faithful to prayer became known as the Giralda, because of its gilded vane.

The base of the campanile measures 50 feet square, and the stone walls, which extend upward for 40 feet, are 9 feet thick. From there up brick is used in the amazingly beautiful geometrical patterns employed by the Moors. As in the Alhambra, the windows are arched over with characteristic horseshoe arches, and all four façades are richly and delicately embroidered in brick.

Through the center of the tower rises a shaft about which winds a spiral ramp, instead of stairs, so that a man on horseback would be able to ascend to the top. Before the Spaniards added the steeple, it is said that four great golden balls were suspended from a crossbar at the minaret's top and that their gleam could be seen for many miles away.

5

5

5

The GREEK SHRINES of Sicily ~

V AGUE traditions make Sicily the island home of the lotus-eaters and the Cyclops. Certain it is that it was inhabited in 1500 B.C. by a race whose bronze implements and pottery relics show great artistic development. Then for 25 centuries a succession of invaders conquered and ruled it, the Greeks, who settled there in 735 B.C., surpassing even their home country in their achievements. There are relics of over 40 Doric shrines in Sicily, and at least two are longer than the Parthenon by more than 100 feet, also of aqueducts, tombs, palaces, superb theatres, and

The ruins of the Temple of Castor and Pollux, the Heavenly Twins, patrons of sport and hospitality, near Girgenti.

battlemented citadels with platforms for catapults.

During a century of peace (750–650 B.C.) the Greeks built their most impressive cities, Girgenti, Selinunte, and Akragas, with their magnificent array of colonnaded bright golden stone buildings. Pindar called Akragas "the most beautiful city of mortals." Its prosperity was largely due to the machinations of a tyrant, Phalaris, who roasted his enemies alive in a brazen bull. But one forgets that as he gazes at those tremendous lofty shrines with their balanced proportions and rich decorations of colored plasters, the sculpture ranging from the primitive naiveté of the earliest Greek art to the graceful perfection of the fifth century. Archæologists consider this work often superior to contemporary work in Greece, for the pioneers in this western outpost expressed themselves with an amazing vigor and beauty.

The GROTTO at Lourdes

THE Grotto at Lourdes in the Pyrenees is the most famous shrine of the contemporary Roman Catholic Church. In itself it is not unusual—merely a small recess fifteen feet deep and fifteen feet wide, where prehistoric remains had been unearthed. But some 80 years ago a mystic virgin, Bernadette Soubirous, sitting in the grotto, beheld the Virgin Mary appearing to her in white with a blue scarf, to say that the waters were sacred and that if the devout would bathe in them they would be healed. Bernadette reported her vision to the village clergy and then retired to a convent for the rest of her life.

The vision was noised about, 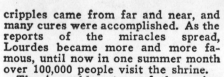 cripples came from far and near, and many cures were accomplished. As the reports of the miracles spread, Lourdes became more and more famous, until now in one summer month over 100,000 people visit the shrine.

The ice-cold waters of the spring have been walled in and flow through taps into a basin over which a statue of the Virgin in white with a blue scarf stands in benediction. This was installed in 1876 with great solemnities, no less than 35 princes of the Church being present. The shrine is crowded with votive offerings and discarded crutches and supports. The throngs who flock there include every condition of suffering and deformity, coming with sublime faith from far-off lands to the Lady of Lourdes in her grotto.

HADRIAN'S VILLA at TIVOLI

IN 125 A.D. Tivoli, fifteen miles from Rome, was a fashionable suburb. The Emperor Hadrian ordered a villa built there for him and for his favorite, a talented youth, Antinous, whose portrait appeared everywhere in statue and plaque. Earthquakes and dampness and centuries of pillage have ruined this estate, but it was once the most magnificent in the ancient world. It was so extensive that they called it "Hadrian's Village," the stonework 600 by 300 yards, the gardens stretching far beyond that.

Huge stone walls, with gates large enough to admit chariots, enclosed the estate. These were so cleverly arranged that at any hour of the day at any season, sunshine or shade was available for the whim of the guests. The distance, a little over a mile, which comprised the walk known as the "constitutional," was marked off at intervals on the walls.

The formal gardens abounded in statuary and pools framed by clipped box and laurel hedges. There were two theatres, a library, and aviary for rare birds, elaborate heated baths, a colony of guest rooms opening onto a central hall, and galleries reproducing Greek and Egyptian palaces, where the Emperor displayed art treasures brought back from his travels.

Here amidst the colorful splendor of rare enamels, marbles, and mosaics, bright contrast to the sombre tones of cypress and olive groves without, Hadrian and Antinous took their ease in luxury appropriate to Roman masters of the world.

Ruins of the Emperor Hadrian's Villa

HADRIAN'S WALL

WHEN Hadrian became emperor in A.D. 117, he determined to put an end to the barbarian raids which kept sweeping down and wiping out Roman garrisons in South Britain. So he planned an elaborate frontier defense, a wall 20 feet high and 8 feet thick, to stretch for 73¼ miles up hill and down dale, across the entire width of the island. At mile intervals were forts armed with catapults, with two smaller watchtowers between, and a path along the top patrolled by guards. On the northern side there were earthworks. On the southern side there was a good road over which supplies could be moved from point to point.

Although builders for centuries have been plundering the stone from the wall, there are enough ruins so that today one can reconstruct the activities along that enormous defense line. The mile forts were well protected by double stone enclosures, with thick wooden, iron-bound doors opening into paved courts, where the ruts of chariot wheels, as in Pompeii, were deeply grooved. There were systematic streets of barracks heated from stone flues, for the Continental recruits were unused to the bitter British winters. There were storehouses, granaries, offices. There were heated baths for the commandants in their private quarters, decorated with carved stone and painted plaster.

This amazingly detailed system was completed in about ten years, and for centuries it held the frontier against barbarian onslaughts.

The Oracle Chamber, with a painted ceiling said to represent the tree of life

The HYPOGEUM, *Malta*

THE huge Hypogeum of Malta is a series of monolithic rooms dug out of solid underground rock during the Neolithic Epoch, probably 3000 years before the dawn of history. They were accidentally discovered by a workman in 1902, and systematic excavations have now restored many of these crude, intercommunicating rooms.

They were arranged in fan shape, the largest one, the Hall, being 21 by 15 feet and about 9 feet high, and the smallest one a mere recess a yard square. They have no regular shape, being primitively laid out, with differing floor levels, sometimes connected by a boulder step. Some of the ceilings are painted red with strange scrollwork. Certain chambers contain basins and niches for ceremonial use.

Because of lack of ventilation and since there are no traces of ashes or food, the conclusion is that these underground burrows were not homes. Quantities of human bones, some perfect, some fragments, some mouldering dust, have been discovered; so scientists assume that the Hypogeum was a huge ossuary. The bones were scraped and dried before being placed in these vaults, for the bones of 200 persons have been discovered in one small cell which would scarcely contain twelve bodies.

Skeletons of fowls, dogs, and pigs, and ornamental pottery indicate that religious rites were celebrated in these crypts. An alabaster nude, fat, short, with curly hair, probably the oldest Venus in existence, was found there, giving some indication of the appearance of that far-off race that dug out the Hypogeum.

The KREMLIN

THERE runs an old proverb: "Above Moscow, the Kremlin; above the Kremlin, Heaven." This ancient citadel, rising from a hill above the Moskwa river, a tributary of the Volga, in the heart of what once was and is now once more the capital of all the Russias, is really a great agglomeration of palaces, churches, monasteries, museums, arsenals, towers, and spires, the whole surrounded by a wall of stone 60 feet high, crowned by 18 towers and pierced by 5 gates.

The Kremlin, once the emblem of the wealth and power of the czars, and now with the tomb of Lenin set against its walls, is still the very heart of Russia. Since the early fourteenth century the land enclosed within the Kremlin's grim walls has been held sacred by all Russians.

Among the famous buildings in the group are the Ivan Véliky tower, 270 feet high, from which one obtains a magnificent view of the many fantastic and gilded towers of half-Asiatic, half-European Moscow; the Savior Gate, built in 1491, over whose portal Czar Alexis suspended a lamp in 1685 and ordered all who passed beneath it to doff their caps under penalty of death; the Cathedral of the Archangel, where many of the czars lie buried; and the jewel-encrusted Cathedral of the Assumption, the foundations of which were laid in 1326.

The Kremlin was practically the only part of the city that escaped the great conflagration started by the patriotic citizens when Napoleon I captured Moscow in 1812.

The LEANING TOWER of PISA

ONE can imagine the consternation of the Pisan architect Bonanno, back in the year 1174, when three stories of his masterpiece, the campanile, now known the world over as the "Leaning Tower of Pisa," were completed and he found that the whole structure was beginning to heel over, as a result of the instability of the subsoil beneath it.

No engineer today would think of digging only ten feet into the ground for a foundation to support such a mass of solid Carrara marble. Instead of pulling it down and starting over, Bonanno went right on, but cleverly diminished the slope of the remaining four stories so as to keep the center of gravity well within the walls.

Today this unique tower with its seven galleries of arches supported by columns, and topped by a smaller story added two centuries later, which contains a chime of bells, is seventeen feet out of the perpendicular. As Dickens says: "It leans as much as the most sanguine tourist could desire."

The tower is round, 180 feet in height, and remains a magnificent example of Romanesque architecture. Its walls at the base are thirteen feet thick. It stands immediately back of the famous marble baptistry and cathedral in the heart of the old city of Pisa, Italy, once the great commercial rival of Venice and Genoa. The great Galileo is said to have taken advantage of the "lean" of the "Leaning Tower" to work out some of his experiments in gravitation.

The MATTERHORN

ABOVE the village of Zermatt, Switzerland, there rises 14,782 feet into the blue the noble pile of gray gneiss and white ice called the Matterhorn. There are higher peaks in the Swiss Alps, but none which so captures the imagination of both native and tourist. From the Italian side one gets the best view, where it looms like a solitary obelisk, its sides as sheer as though they had been sliced off by a giant knife. The Swiss side has a gentler slope.

On two sides the peak is swathed in glaciers—on the Swiss side by Leichenbretten, which means "boards for carrying the dead." On the Italian side is the Linceul, or "winding sheet."

Matterhorn, down whose slopes frequent avalanches crash and thunder, long resisted the attempts of puny man to reach its summit. Not until July, 1865, did the Whymper party conquer this noble peak, and then only at the cost of three of its members.

Geologists will tell you that Matterhorn, or Mount Cervin, as the French call it, is the butt end of a spur, or ridge, which dwindles into the Italian foothills to the south. And so there are no peaks near by to detract from its grandeur. To one who has beheld it at sunset, with its sides washed in a glow of vermilion and mauve, the sight will ever remain a dream come true.

MONT ST. MICHEL

ACCORDING to Celtic mythology, Mont St. Michel was a sea tomb whither the souls of the dead were ferried in an invisible bark. Later, in the year 708 A.D., when Saint Michael, the saint of high places, appeared in a vision to the Bishop of Avranches, he commanded an oratory to be built upon the granite islet which rises 260 feet above the sea off the coast of Normandy. And so it became a shrine to which pilgrims came to worship, just as today tourists come to view the same ancient stronghold which played such a gallant part in French history.

Here Richard Cœur de Lion founded a monastery and collected the ships with which he landed in England in the twelfth century. Here only, when Henry V of England, hero of Agincourt, swarmed over Normandy, were the invaders beaten off after three desperate sieges. Two bombards, still preserved near the town gate, are reminders of the last assault in 1434. Here ancient dungeons and crypts, dating from the eleventh century, testify to the days when the islet was a prison, monastery, and fortress in one.

A mile-long causeway now joins the island to the mainland, and at low tide its granite cone is surrounded by sand flats. Around its base is a circlet of mediæval walls and towers, while along the single steep street straggle the quaint old houses, rising tier on tier as though plastered against the rock. An ancient abbey crowns the whole, its huge buttresses and bastians flanking a central bell tower and spire.

The MOSQUE of ST. SOPHIA

THE terraced cluster of St. Sophia's domes overlooks Constantinople from the highest of her seven hills. This supreme example of Byzantine art was built by order of the Emperor Justinian between 532 and 537 A.D. He determined to rear a temple which would excel all others, and he himself supervised the work daily. When he surveyed its completed massive beauty, he ordered a statue of a chagrined Solomon placed before it, for he exclaimed: "O Solomon, I have surpassed your temple!"

The exterior is simple but tremendous, a pile of small domes topped by a magnificent master dome upheld by 40 windows. The architect Anthemius made a daring experiment when he placed the 110-foot round dome 180 feet high over the square space where the arms of the church met. Twenty years later it crashed from its dizzy height, but a new and higher cupola was then successfully built.

In contrast to the severity of the exterior is the highly decorated interior, a rainbow of dazzling color. The church is in the form of a Greek cross, and the first impression is one of the vast bright distances of the mighty transepts, and the richly tinted spaces of the soaring dome. Marbles of every hue from all over the world form the pillars, walls, and mosaic ceilings and floors. When the Turks transformed it into a Mohammedan mosque, they whitewashed over the gorgeous Christian scenes on its walls.

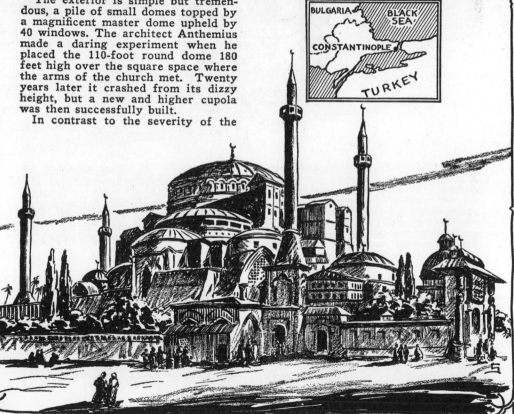

The OLYMPIAN JUPITER

IN THE holy grove of the quiet vale of Olympia in 460 B.C. the Greeks dedicated an altar to the twelve gods, the very center of which was to be a great statue of Zeus, "whose power surpasses that of gods and men." The genius Pheidias and his pupils were to erect the temple with Corinthian columns and to spare no cost or materials in the statue. When their work was complete, it was so magnificent that the Olympian Jupiter became one of the Seven Wonders of the World.

In 408 B.C. the temple and statue were destroyed by fire, but before then many travellers had described it accurately and many artists had reproduced it faithfully on coins.

Zeus was a benignant and majestic seated figure, the flesh executed of iron, the flowing locks and robes and sandals of gold, the eyes of lambent gems. The sceptre was crowned with an eagle sparkling with jewels. The throne was of blue, and ranged about it were 29 lesser gods, portrayed in struggles and victories.

As the half-open temple was damp, the statue was frequently washed with oil, and the channels which carried this away may still be seen in the floor.

The ancients wrote that the beautiful figure expressed such a serenity that it calmed and soothed all who beheld it, making them forget the crushing load of human life in the vast peace of immortality.

The PARTHENON

HIGH above Athens, dominating the city, stands that beautiful, serene, and majestic temple which epitomizes the best in Greek art, the Parthenon. Pericles dedicated it about 445 B.C. to the city's virgin goddess of wisdom, Athene, and the mammoth ivory and gold statue of her which it once contained was its glory.

The architects, Iktinos and Kallikrates, planned the building, including the Doric colonnade. There were four divisions, the inner shrine for Athene's statue, the Parthenon proper for housing the temple gear, a front portico with iron grill for sacrifices, and a grilled rear portico for the fabulous treasures listed by stone inscriptions on the walls. This was all of the most gleaming white marble, now weathered to a rich gold, and elaborately ornamented with polychrome decorations, dazzlingly brilliant in the clear Athens air.

But the most beautiful feature was the sculptured frieze by Pheidas. All about the building, within the colonnade, he carved a procession in honor of Athene, so arranged that as one viewed it in the sun and shadow falling between the columns, it seemed actually to be moving.

The Parthenon survived many vicissitudes, until in 1687 the Turks used it for a powder magazine and its center was blown out. Afterwards most of the marbles were taken to the British Museum, so that now that loveliest shrine is stark and empty, a phantom memory of a glorious perfection.

The BURIED CITY of POMPEII

POMPEII is one of the most romantic spots in the world, for an eruption of Vesuvius buried it in 79 A.D. under 20 feet of ashes, which sealed it for centuries. Then in 1748, systematic excavations revealed every detail of the ancient city.

The old volcano must have given warning, for many citizens had fled, but some 2000 have been found just as they were caught at the instant of death. The rich died waiting to be feasted in a red and black frescoed dining room, where couches were drawn up to the carved table. The poor died hurrying to put up the shutters of their little open shops. The devout died in the temple, vainly striving to save the altar treasures. Unruly gladiators died where they had been pilloried in stocks just outside the amphitheatre. In one cellar 20 persons cowered together for safety.

In the shops the stocks of dried fish, vegetables, and cereals are still in glass bottles on the shelves. The tavern has some wine jars standing in the earth to cool, while others are over braziers to be heated. The surgeon's office is outfitted with elaborate bronze tools. Over the doorways of the stucco houses, practically windowless to keep out the heat, is the sign to avert the evil eye. On the brick walls along main streets are scrawled political lampoons.

So a sudden catastrophe preserved for all time the life of an early Roman town.

PLAN OF POMPEII

STREET OF ABUNDANCE, AS RESTORED.

The City of Rosetta

The ROSETTA STONE

THE Rosetta Stone, carefully cherished by the British Museum, is merely a shapeless broken slab of black basalt inscribed with messages in three different characters. Yet it furnished the key which unlocked the secrets of 4000 years of Egyptian records. Without it explorers would not have found many of the wonders of ancient Egypt and could not have understood what they did find

Young and Champollion were the two Egyptologists who finally deciphered the writings and wrote an Egyptian grammar from their findings. The Rosetta Stone is three feet nine inches by two feet four inches in size; its inscription is cut in two languages, Greek and Egyptian, and in three scripts, Greek, and the Egyptian hieroglyphic and demotic. The last is a sort of shorthand developed about 900 B.C. The messages are identical —a copy of a decree sent out by Egyptian priests, ordering the commemoration of the coronation of King Ptolemy V Epiphanes in his ninth year, 196 B.C., and enumerating the good deeds of his reign.

It was originally set up at Memphis, but was later moved to Rosetta, a seaport where Boussard, one of Napoleon's officers, found it in 1799.

It was the bilingual character that gave the clue to its value, and beginning with the royal names, each enclosed in a cartouche, and working from the Greek version, an Egyptian alphabet was finally construed from which early manuscripts could be deciphered.

ROSETTA STONE

IN 67 A.D. St. Peter was martyred on the Vatican Hill in Rome and buried there. The spot immediately became sacred, and in 313 Emperor Constantine set it apart as property of the Christian Church and built a basilica over the holy tomb. The church grew increasingly important, until the present St. Peter's Cathedral replaced the original basilica and became the first church of the Roman Catholic faith. The actual tomb, covered with a 150-pound gold cross presented by Empress Helena, is now sealed in the crypt, and together with some fragments of mosaic pavement is all that remains of Constantine's Basilica.

But the great St. Peter's which rises above it is the largest and most impressive cathedral in the world. A wide-spreading plaza with a majestic double circle of 284 pillars stretches before it, affording an unobstructed view of its tremendous proportions.

Michelangelo was architect and decorator for the famous dome, the loftiest in the world. It dominates the city, and from the interior the great reaches of its colored circle raised high over the spacious transepts are awe-inspiring and almost boundless.

Bramante designed the vaulting of choir and nave, and Bernini added an elaborate loggia, using the bronze of the Pantheon in its construction. The coloring and carving are so intricate as to be almost baroque. The holy water bowls are as large as baths. Yet the cathedral is so unbelievably vast that it seems empty, suggesting infinite and magnificent space.

Entrance
to tunnel

SWITZERLAND

BRIGUE Simplon
        Tunnel ISELLE

I T A L Y

DIAGRAM SHOWING HEIGHT
OF MOUNTAINS THROUGH
WHICH TUNNEL PASSES   MONT LEONE
                            3561
3000   2135   3000
                          Lago d'Avine
2000   Rosswald   2238   Pte del Teggiola 2000
          Berisal
1000
Brigue 686   T U N N E L   684 Iselle

IN 1898, seventeen years after the first train roared through the St. Gothard tunnel under the Alps that lie between Switzerland and Italy, engineers began work upon an even greater bore, 7000 feet beneath the carriage road which Napoleon had built a century before over the Simplon Pass.

The St. Gothard is nine and one-half miles long and built in the shape of a figure eight, while the Simplon's twin bores, each sixteen feet wide by nineteen feet high, are three miles longer and run straight through the heart of the Alps from Brigue, Switzerland, to Iselle, Italy. The rock temperature midway through the tunnel even in winter is 130 degrees, but is kept down to 89 degrees by spraying devices. So terrific is the pressure from the weight above, that the floor is kept from buckling only by heavy masonry inverts.

During the construction, which was completed in 1905, a great spring of cold water was struck two miles from the Iselle portal, which poured 10,000 gallons a minute into the bore. Later a spring of boiling hot water near the other portal was tapped, gushing forth at the rate of 2000 gallons to the minute, necessitating abandonment of the work for a time.

Thanks to the progress in engineering and better ventilation, the Simplon cost the lives of only 60 men in seven years, while the St. Gothard took a total of 800 in eight years.

STONEHENGE

IT WAS probably 2000 B.C. when the strange gigantic open temple was set up at Stonehenge. The stones are so heavy and the site so lonely that they have since remained practically undisturbed by mankind, and though several of the trilithons have fallen and broken and much is just a tumbled mass of rock, still a fairly accurate reconstruction can be worked out from the remains.

The spot was sacred and surrounded by burial mounds. The shrine itself was a series of concentric circles about a horseshoe of master stones, opening towards a gigantic boulder, called the Friar's Heel. The sun rises over this in midsummer, and the formation suggests sun worship. Between the great stone and the open temple lies the Slaughtering Stone, a vast slab used for sacrifices.

The main earthwork was 300 feet in diameter, marked by stones at regular intervals. The second circle formed a crude tremendous fence of upright stones, 25 to 30 feet high, supporting horizontal slabs which were jointed firmly into place in an amazingly advanced fashion.

The third circle was of "mystery stones," so called because they are of a type foreign to that locality and must have been brought from a great distance, no one knows how. The inner horeshoe of mammoth detached slabs pointed to the Friar's Heel.

Archæologists have found the tools by which this massive monument was assembled—crude picks of red deer's antlers, flint hammers, stone chisels—poor help to the ancient people who performed the herculean task of building and arranging those giant circles.

RECONSTRUCTION

STONEHENGE LIES SIX MILES DISTANT FROM SALISBURY

The STRASBOURG (Strassburg) CLOCK

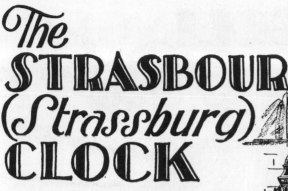

THE famous astronomical clock in the Strasbourg Cathedral (twenty feet high) is so ingenious a mechanism that crowds gather every day at the striking of the hours to see its performances.

It was begun in 1571 to replace an earlier clock of which nothing remains but the cock which emerges to flap its wings, stretch its neck, and crow.

Conradus Dasypodius, professor of mathematics at Strasbourg, completed this most wonderful clock in three years, persisting in his work although he became totally blind before he had it ready for the cathedral façade.

Its tricks vary with the passing of the minutes, of the hours, and even of the days and seasons, for it is connected with the chimes, and rings appropriate tunes at festival seasons. It controls a globe of the heavens wherein the daily motion of the earth is shown, the sun runs its course every year, and the moon every 28 days. Two circles show the yearly calendar and the century calendar, with the year movable feasts, eclipses, and quantities of other data.

The passing of the days is shown by a horse-drawn chariot, while other quaint figures mark the quarters and the minutes, a host of characters of all ages, from children to old men, showing endless ingenuity and invention.

The clock has been struck by lightning several times, but has been running steadily since 1852, the marvel of all who behold its naïve but nevertheless remarkable feats.

STROMBOLI

SINCE the fourth century B.C., when mention was first made of Stromboli, sailors have known this continuously active volcano as the "Lighthouse of the Mediterranean." It is situated upon one of a group of volcanic islands known as the Lipari, off the coast of Sicily. According to mythology, here dwelt Aiolos, lord of the winds, whose stronghold Ulysses twice visited. During the Punic War these islands served as a naval base for the Carthaginians, and later the Romans.

Geologists fairly definitely have traced the history of this volcanic mountain which rises 3000 feet above the level of the sea, more than half of its bulk being under water. Centuries ago the ocean's bed at a spot off Sicily's coast gave way with a terrific explosion, sending up a great column of rock and ashes and sea water. When the giant tidal waves had died away on distant shores, there stood the mountain-island as it stands today. From its fissures the lava has never ceased to flow, and over it hangs the ominous cloud of smoke, lighted from beneath by the red-hot lava.

The principal crater is located part way down the slope of the cone, so that observers standing above may look down into the seething cauldron and watch the ceaseless activity taking place below. There are several smaller craters, or "blowholes," which contribute their showers of lava fragments to the continuous show provided by the "Lighthouse of the Mediterranean."

A mountain pierced by a natural tunnel

TORGHATTEN, NORWAY

FAR back in the Glacial period, so geologists say, two great ice caps, or glaciers, one moving westward from Russia across the Baltic, the other sweeping eastward across the Atlantic, met and strove against each other in the high valleys of Norway. After centuries, the terrific grinding and erosion ceased. The ice melted and left those high valleys submerged. Only the lofty peaks remained to form the walls of the drowned valleys, or fjords, or as steep, rocky islets off the rugged coast.

There are literally hundreds of thousands of these Norwegian islands, but the most famous one is the Torghatten in the province of Nord-land. This bare mass of rock, 800 feet high, gets its name from its shape, which resembles a Norwegian market hat.

As one approaches it, one sees high up on its escarpment a square hole, like a window. So perfectly has the tunnelling been done, that it looks as though the hand of man had executed it, but this window 400 feet above the level of the sea is just another bit of evidence of that age-old battle of the waves of ice. On one side the tunnel mouth is 64 feet high, on the other 250 feet, while its length is over 500 feet. A giant machine-chisel could have made no cleaner job than that icy drill of millions of years ago.

ENGLAND
Thames river
LONDON
ENGLISH CHANNEL

Tower Bridge in background

The TOWER of LONDON

THE spot most typically British in all England, perhaps, is Tower Hill, on the north bank of the Thames in London, where stands that eleventh century Norman stronghold, the Tower of London. The original foundations beneath the twelve acres of walls and towers which once housed the courts of the Plantagenet kings and whose stones are soaked with the blood of so many English prisoners, including three of Henry VIII's queens, date back to the days of the Roman invasion.

Around the outer castellated wall with its massive flanking towers rising at intervals is a moat, once filled from the Thames, but long since dry.

A second fortification, called the Ballium Wall, even loftier, with thirteen towers (one of which is Wakefield Tower, where the crown jewels are kept and where Henry VI met his death while at prayers) forms an inner wall. In the center of all rises the great keep, or donjon, known as the White Tower, erected in the time of William the Conqueror. Here Sir Walter Raleigh was once kept prisoner. It now houses a magnificent collection of armor.

On the Thames side, between St. Thomas' Tower and the Bloody Tower, is the famous Traitors' Gate, through which so many hapless prisoners went to their doom.

TRAJAN'S COLUMN

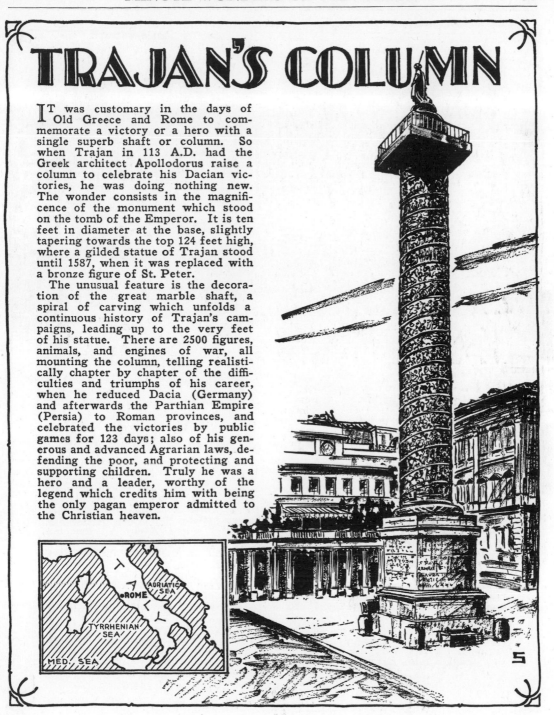

IT was customary in the days of Old Greece and Rome to commemorate a victory or a hero with a single superb shaft or column. So when Trajan in 113 A.D. had the Greek architect Apollodorus raise a column to celebrate his Dacian victories, he was doing nothing new. The wonder consists in the magnificence of the monument which stood on the tomb of the Emperor. It is ten feet in diameter at the base, slightly tapering towards the top 124 feet high, where a gilded statue of Trajan stood until 1587, when it was replaced with a bronze figure of St. Peter.

The unusual feature is the decoration of the great marble shaft, a spiral of carving which unfolds a continuous history of Trajan's campaigns, leading up to the very feet of his statue. There are 2500 figures, animals, and engines of war, all mounting the column, telling realistically chapter by chapter of the difficulties and triumphs of his career, when he reduced Dacia (Germany) and afterwards the Parthian Empire (Persia) to Roman provinces, and celebrated the victories by public games for 123 days; also of his generous and advanced Agrarian laws, defending the poor, and protecting and supporting children. Truly he was a hero and a leader, worthy of the legend which credits him with being the only pagan emperor admitted to the Christian heaven.

The VATICAN

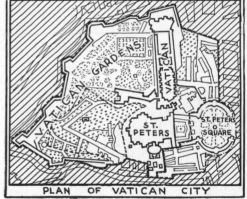

PLAN OF VATICAN CITY

THE Vatican is the name given to the group of buildings clustered on the hill about St. Peter's at Rome, and is the very heart of the Roman Catholic Church and the residence of its ruler. From the days when Constantine built a basilica over St. Peter's tomb, the popes came frequently to celebrate feasts at this sacred spot, and it grew necessary to provide residences where they and their retinues might be housed overnight. A most lavish series of palaces and chapels were built, all set in the extensive Vatican gardens with cypress and yew hedges and handsome sculptures. Nicholas V in the fifteenth century did more than any other pope to have these residences rival the imperial palaces of the world. Now St. Peter's and the Vatican Palace together form the greatest continuous building in existence.

There are seven divisions of the Vatican, all beautifully decorated by the finest Renaissance artists: the pontifical palace, Sistine and Pauline chapels, picture galleries, Nicholas V's library, museums, outbuildings and barracks, and the gardens with the Pope's Casino.

There are 11,000 rooms, with only male attendants, including the famous Swiss Guard, who still wear the blue and gold uniforms designed by Michelangelo.

Against the regal background of these magnificent palaces the Pope and his household move with all the pomp and ceremony of the Middle Ages.

VESUVIUS

AT THE time of Jesus, Vesuvius was a beautiful green mountain, rising 4267 feet above the plain of Campania, about ten miles from the Bay of Naples. Its sides were covered with forests and vineyards and peaceful gardens.

Then in 63 A.D. began a series of convulsions, rumblings, and earthquakes, which alarmed the natives but did not frighten them away.

In 79 A.D. a huge black cloud soared suddenly out of the quiet crater, and soon a tremendous explosion blew off the top of the mountain, devastating the surprised countryside. Pompeii, a populous city at its base, was buried under 20 feet of loose ashes. Herculaneum, another beautiful city, was covered with a torrent of mud. The elder Pliny, who was commanding a Roman fleet at Misenum, sailed to rescue any survivors of the sudden catastrophe; but he was himself suffocated by poisonous fumes as he approached the bay.

Periodically since 79 A.D. this treacherous mountain has rained hot mud, burning ashes, molten lava, and torrents of boiling water out upon the surrounding country. In 472 there was an explosion which spread ashes as far as Constantinople. In 1779 great boulders were hurled to tremendous heights above the crater, while rivers of red hot lava boiled down its sides.

Now Vesuvius is never completely quiescent, but from time to time emits steam, deadly gases, showers of rocks and lava, as if to remind the world of the destruction of its past and warn it to beware of its future.

FROM NAPLES

WESTMINSTER ABBEY, London

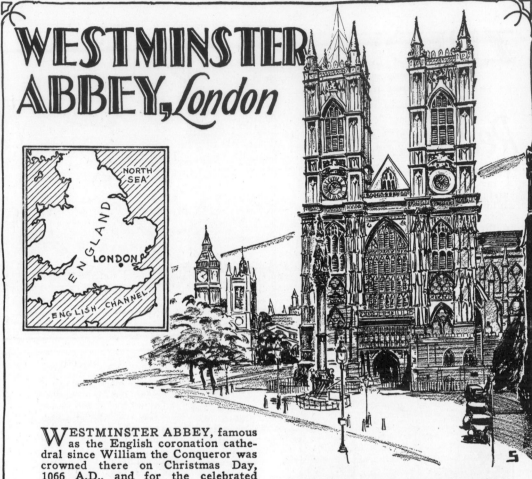

WESTMINSTER ABBEY, famous as the English coronation cathedral since William the Conqueror was crowned there on Christmas Day, 1066 A.D., and for the celebrated tombs which it shelters, was originally built in 616 A.D. in honor of St. Peter and called "the Collegiate Church of St. Peter." Its present name comes from the Benedictine monastery at first connected with it, known as the "Western Monastery" or "Minster of the West." This was destroyed by the Danish invasion, but as Edward the Confessor's piety was especially devoted to St. Peter, he began restorations in 1050 and left great sums to further the work after his death. Henry III, often called its second founder, in 1220, at fifteen years of age, laid the foundation for the lady chapel and inaugurated the custom of using Westminster as the mausoleum for English royalty.

During the days of the Reformation its career was troubled. First the monastery was dissolved and the abbot converted into a dean. Then Roman services were resumed, until Edward VI replaced Mass by Communion, and the brass lecterns, candlesticks, angels, and sumptuous vestments were sold to provide a library. Mary reinstated the monastery, only to have it abolished by Elizabeth.

Though Sir Christopher Wren redecorated the towers and exterior, the abbey in general has remained unchanged through the long centuries.

ZUIDER ZEE Reclamation~

IN THE new geographies one familiar name will be missing which has intrigued many generations of school-children—the Zuider Zee.

Six hundred and fifty years, almost to the day, after the sea in the year 1282 had swept in over the sandy spit which once connected North Holland and Friesland and turned an inland lake into a salty arm of the sea, the Zuider Zee once again became a saline inland lake. For in the spring of 1932 the huge seventeen-mile barring dam across the mouth of the Zuider Zee, leaving the placid Yssel

THE BARRING DAM MAKES A PLACID LAKE ~

Lake in its place, had become a reality.

This dam, 300 feet wide, carrying two wide main traffic roads, a cyclist path, and a railroad, has been completed at a cost of $50,000,000. Great locks near each end make it possible to regulate the water level of the new lake. The master plan, on which work began in 1924, calls for the enclosing dike described above and the draining of the lake, thereby eventually adding 550,000 acres of new fertile ground to the domain of the Dutch people.

The project has been divided into polders, as shown on the map, around each of which smaller dikes are built and the water pumped out. The first polder, the northwest, comprising 50,-000 acres, is already complete and crops are being raised upon it, while roads and villages are in process of construction. Work is now going forward on the second, or northeast polder, covering 132,000 acres, which will require fifteen more years to complete.

A SCENE ALONG THE ZUIDER ZEE

Asia

EUROPE

AFRICA

PACIFIC OCEAN

ARABIAN SEA

BAY OF BENGAL

INDIAN OCEAN

EQUATOR

EQUATOR

RHODES
MAUSOLEUM of HALICARNASSUS
JERICHO, Wall
JERUSALEM, Wailing Wall
PETRA
BEHISTUN, Rock of
MESHED
BAGDAD, White Palace of Ctesiphon
BABYLON, Hanging Gardens
PERSEPOLIS, Ruins
MECCA, The Kaaba
MESHED
Diwan-i-Khas, Great Mosque, DELHI
MAHAL
FATTEHPUR
AKBARS TOMB
BENARES
BUDDH-GAYA
GREAT BANYAN TREE
BOMBAY
Parsee Towers of Silence
GOLCONDA
ELLORA Rock Temples
MYSORE Colossal
DAGOBAS
LION PALACE
LHASA Potala Palace Tashi Lama
MOUNT EVEREST
PAGAN, Temples
BINGY CAVES
SHWE-DAGON
Wat Phra Keo,
Wat Po,
BANGKOK
ANGKOR
WALL
MING TOMBS
PORCELAIN PAGODA
NIKKO
FUJIYAMA
KYOTO Temple of 33,333 Gods

SKRENDA

AKBAR'S TOMB, Sikandra

DURING his long and prosperous reign, the great Moghul emperor, who died in 1605, built himself an elaborate tomb, a veritable palace, three stories of red sandstone surmounted by a fourth of dazzling white marble, all set in an oriental garden enclosed by an ornate wall with beautiful pierced and fretted gates.

During his life this palace-tomb was the rendezvous for his friends, and the most exotic revelries and feasts were enjoyed on that upper story, in the center of which stood the magnificent white marble cenotaph, uncovered, open to the blue sky and the tropic dews. It was lavishly carved and bore the motto, "God Is Greatest," for Akbar was a liberal who tolerated all creeds. Nearby stood a small marble gold-covered pillar, in which one of the gems of Akbar's world-renowned jewel collection, the "Koh-i-noor diamond," was kept for 130 years, until the Shah Nadir of Persia carried it away.

At Akbar's death the tomb immediately ceased to be a center for festivities and became consecrated and silent. The actual body of the Emperor was not placed in the elaborate mausoleum of the embellished upper story, but according to Moghul custom, directly below it on the simple first story, where a plain doorway and narrow passage lead to the undecorated vault in which the greatest of Moghul emperors rests beneath a simple marble slab bare of all inscription.

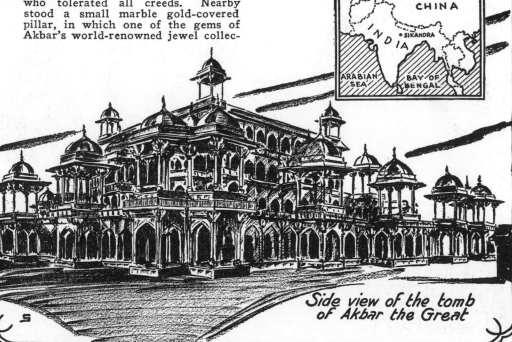

Side view of the tomb of Akbar the Great

ANGKOR VAT

ANGKOR,
the mystery of the jungle

ISOLATED miles inland in Siam lie the majestic ruins of Angkor, strangling with vegetation, deserted save for some yellow-robed Buddhist priests. What race could have become powerful enough to create these superb temples and then vanish completely, leaving no other trace? It was probably the Khmer Empire, which rose in the fifth century, but was unaccountably wiped out by the tenth. They were serpent worshippers, and everywhere one comes upon the snake motif in the decoration, the erect cowl of a cobra, or the seven-headed sacred naga rising from a pool, or forming a long balustrade, its body supported by hundreds of squat figures, and its fan-shaped head the newel.

Angkor Vat is the most beautiful of the many temples, a vast pile of volcanic stone, fitted without cement, with walls and moats, with long flights of stairs, with colonnades and cloisters, with conical towers and vaulted roofs. Every inch of the in-terior is carved with bas-reliefs, literally acres of them, with scarcely a repetition of detail, rhythmic and realistic dancing girls, twisting serpents, slashing warriors, all writhing motion, in contrast to the apathy of the great ruin gradually sinking into the jungle.

When one asks the few natives of the place, whose highest architectural accomplishment is a loose bamboo shed, "Who built the temple?," they stare at that exquisite marvel in stone and reply, "The Gods."

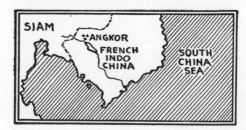

The BINGYI CAVES, Burma

THERE are five remarkable series of caves in the vicinity of Moulmein, of which the Bingyi Caves are perhaps the most picturesque. Strangely isolated limestone hills rise abruptly from the plains near the Dondami River, and here the sea in prehistoric times dug out these weird caverns, grotesquely hung with stalactites and stalagmites. The entrance is reached by a climb of 100 feet after crossing a boiling hot pool.

The caves are filled with pagodas and shrines, and every ledge holds a Buddha, all dressed in monk's robes, with his curly hair knotted on top of his head, the lobes of his ears stretched out to meet his shoulders. Evidently the Bingyi Caves have been sacred for centuries, for these Buddhas, and the fragments of hundreds which have been destroyed through the years, represent every period and age. There are many manuscripts, too, and terra cotta tablets recounting Burmese history, which show that precious relics have been sent here to be cared for by the priests since time immemorial.

The devout have ever flocked to these weird caves to pray to the Buddhas, even though until recent years they were swarming with myriads of bats, the floor in places several feet deep with their dead bodies and droppings. Now they have been cleaned and strongly lighted, so that even the main cave, very deep and dark, containing a huge pool and a large pagoda, is available for prayers and picnics, a favorite combination with the Burmese.

The COLOSSUS of MYSORE

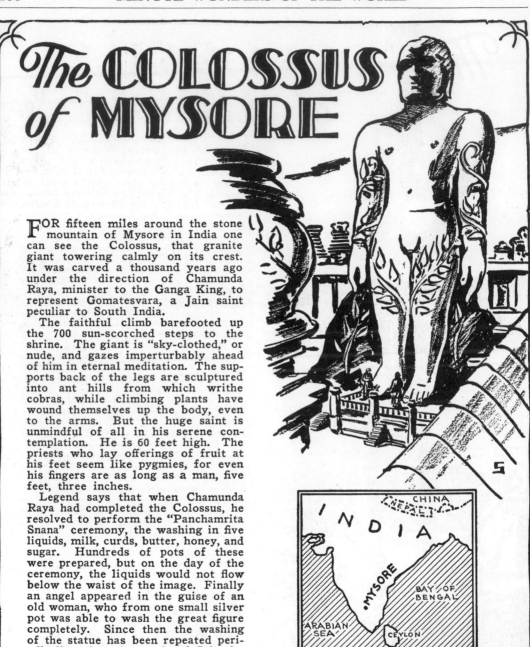

FOR fifteen miles around the stone mountain of Mysore in India one can see the Colossus, that granite giant towering calmly on its crest. It was carved a thousand years ago under the direction of Chamunda Raya, minister to the Ganga King, to represent Gomatesvara, a Jain saint peculiar to South India.

The faithful climb barefooted up the 700 sun-scorched steps to the shrine. The giant is "sky-clothed," or nude, and gazes imperturbably ahead of him in eternal meditation. The supports back of the legs are sculptured into ant hills from which writhe cobras, while climbing plants have wound themselves up the body, even to the arms. But the huge saint is unmindful of all in his serene contemplation. He is 60 feet high. The priests who lay offerings of fruit at his feet seem like pygmies, for even his fingers are as long as a man, five feet, three inches.

Legend says that when Chamunda Raya had completed the Colossus, he resolved to perform the "Panchamrita Snana" ceremony, the washing in five liquids, milk, curds, butter, honey, and sugar. Hundreds of pots of these were prepared, but on the day of the ceremony, the liquids would not flow below the waist of the image. Finally an angel appeared in the guise of an old woman, who from one small silver pot was able to wash the great figure completely. Since then the washing of the statue has been repeated periodically, when thousands of Jain devotees make the pilgrimage to Mysore.

The COLOSSUS of RHODES

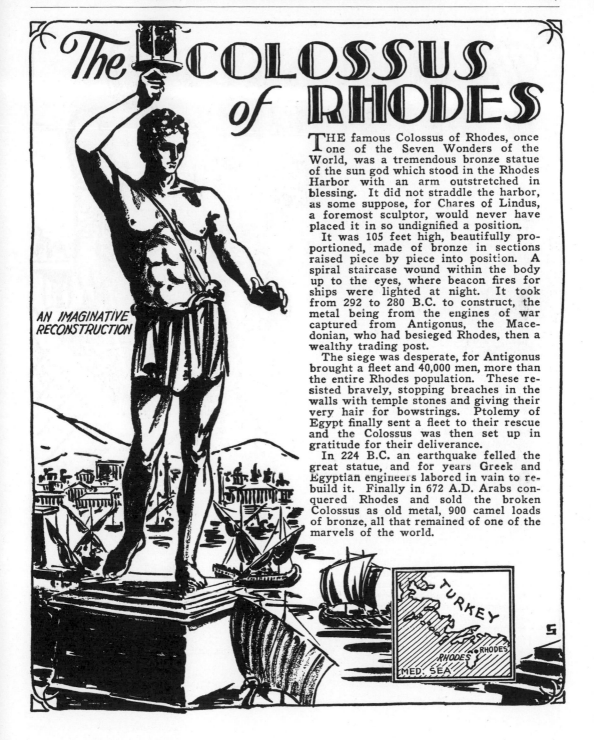

AN IMAGINATIVE RECONSTRUCTION

THE famous Colossus of Rhodes, once one of the Seven Wonders of the World, was a tremendous bronze statue of the sun god which stood in the Rhodes Harbor with an arm outstretched in blessing. It did not straddle the harbor, as some suppose, for Chares of Lindus, a foremost sculptor, would never have placed it in so undignified a position.

It was 105 feet high, beautifully proportioned, made of bronze in sections raised piece by piece into position. A spiral staircase wound within the body up to the eyes, where beacon fires for ships were lighted at night. It took from 292 to 280 B.C. to construct, the metal being from the engines of war captured from Antigonus, the Macedonian, who had besieged Rhodes, then a wealthy trading post.

The siege was desperate, for Antigonus brought a fleet and 40,000 men, more than the entire Rhodes population. These resisted bravely, stopping breaches in the walls with temple stones and giving their very hair for bowstrings. Ptolemy of Egypt finally sent a fleet to their rescue and the Colossus was then set up in gratitude for their deliverance.

In 224 B.C. an earthquake felled the great statue, and for years Greek and Egyptian engineers labored in vain to rebuild it. Finally in 672 A.D. Arabs conquered Rhodes and sold the broken Colossus as old metal, 900 camel loads of bronze, all that remained of one of the marvels of the world.

RUANWELI DAGOBA, at ANURADHAPURA.

The DAGOBAS of CEYLON

AFTER Buddhism made the building of shrines a sacred duty, Ceylon became filled with countless dagobas. These are rounded domes of millions of bricks piled over a sacred relic. In one case the relic is a hair from the left eyebrow of Buddha. In the very sacred though small dagoba of Thuparama, surrounded by a circle of granite columns, the saint's right collarbone has been guarded since 247 B.C.

The most sacred of the larger dagobas is Ruanweli, with a secret chamber which only monks may enter and whose relic is unknown. Its foundation was formed of earth trampled down by the feet of elephants encased in leathern pads. This beaten earth supported limestone terraces from which rose the great dome 270 feet high. At the four corners were four guarding Buddhas.

One king, when it was first built, laid bricks and vessels of gold and silver before it; so it was called Ruanweli, Gold Dust. Another king ordered its huge dome entirely covered with red clay into which fresh fragrant flowers were stuck, until it resembled a giant bouquet. A third is said to have honored it by throwing "a net of diamonds" over its great surface.

It is not so cared for now. Tropic vegetation has been allowed to creep into the joints between the bricks, spreading them and cracking the dome, relentlessly going about the work of breaking down the famous shrine which has been sacred for centuries.

The DIWAN-I-KHAS, DELHI

IN THE magnificent palace at Delhi which Shah Jehan built in the 17th century there is one room which outshines every other in India and possibly in the whole world. It is the Diwan-i-Khas, the Hall of Audience, built of alabaster set with jewels, its many-arched ceiling upheld by a forest of square marble pillars, panelled and inlaid. They are sometimes white, sometimes ivory, sometimes old gold in tint, but always glittering with a million precious gems forming infinitely beautiful designs of flowers and trees and mosaics. It is thought that Austin de Bordeaux, a talented but renegade French jeweller, wrought these decorations while he was exiled in India. Certainly, only the cunning hand of a master could have produced this unbelievable and unequalled beauty.

A long marble base once supported the famous Peacock Throne, more of a bed than a seat, made of solid gold incrusted with rubies, diamonds, and sapphires. Two peacocks with gorgeously spread tails stood behind it, and in the center of the back was a life-size parrot cut from a single emerald. This jewel, the most valuable in the world, was stolen by the Nadir Shah in the eighteenth century, but the beautiful casket which held it is still there.

Over the entrance arch the architect inscribed these words, the most fitting description of the exquisite Diwan-i-Khas: "If Heaven there be on the face of the earth, it is here, it is here, it is here."

FUJIYAMA, sacred mountain of JAPAN

FUJIYAMA, sacred mountain of Japan, is held holy by all of its innumerable sects, regardless of how far they may differ on other points. Its beautiful snow-capped peak appears over and over again in their prints and their pottery. Every Japanese reveres it and if possible climbs at least once the arduous and toilsome 12,000 feet to its top to look into its lofty crater. It is a difficult ascent, and the Japanese proverb reads: "There are two kinds of fools, those who have never ascended Fuji and those who have ascended twice."

Tradition says the mountain was suddenly upheaved during a single night in 285 B.C. It was an active volcano long ago, but has been quiescent since 1707, its slopes green with trees and grass, and its graceful cone snow-capped the year round. It is a lonely peak, and its majesty is emphasized because it rises solitary above the sea.

So universally is it loved that the ideal feminine forehead is called "Fuji bitai," for it must be white and shapely and smoothly rising like the sacred mountain.

The Buddhists call it the "Peak of the White Lotus," for to them it is the symbol of the flower which grows with green leaves at its foot to raise a cup of breathless white to the sky. So about Fujiyama is there an air of infinite purity and peace which transcends earth and points to heaven. No wonder the Japanese revere it as holy.

The GANGES at BENARES

BENARES is the most sacred city of Northern India, the very center of its ardent worship of Siva, the Hindu god who is the destroyer and rebuilder of life, the emblem of pitiless and endless change, controller of the whole circle of existence. There it is that thousands of pilgrims travel every year to bathe in the holy waters of the Ganges, which is said to spring from Siva's head and which flows down from the Himalayas, Siva's home. The water is greenish and thick with mountain mud, filled with remnants of flower offerings and funeral ashes; and thousands of men, women, and children of all conditions bathe in this mixture of impurity daily, believing that they will thus be cleansed from disease and sin. The huge tank of Pischamochan or "Deliverance from Demons" is supposed to be especially efficacious, and is always crowded with joyous, faithful, and very dirty Hindus.

The famous Burning Ghats are on the bank of the holy river. Here the corpses of the dead, wrapped in winding sheets, are tenderly laid on pyres and covered with a few logs. An ordinary funeral of wood costs five dollars, but if the relatives of the departed want a fire of dried cow dung and oil the price is less. A consecrated person of special caste then applies the sacred fire and in half an hour the charred ashes are scattered in the placid river, which, according to Hindu belief, will carry the soul to eternal peace. Brahmin and Buddhist, alike, believe Benares to be nearer heaven than any other place on earth.

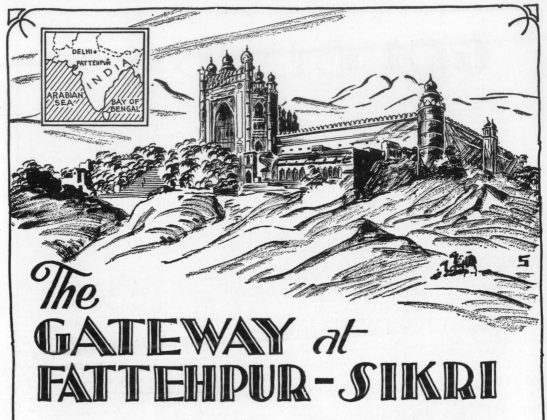

The GATEWAY at FATTEHPUR-SIKRI

THE splendid palace of Fattehpur-Sikri in India, once the favorite abode of the great Emperor Akbar, is deserted now, but the beautiful entrance gate, considered one of the most magnificent arches in the world, still stands intact. Tradition says that as the Mohammedan prince was returning home from a conquest with his Hindu wife, grieving over the death of twin children, they rested at this lonely spot. A holy man came to them and prophesied that if they would but build a palace there, a son, Jehangir, would be born to them.

So Akbar built Fattehpur-Sikri of the red sandstone of the hill, the buildings, even the mosque, showing a decided Hindu influence in honor of his beloved wife. The gateway is a triumphal arch, larger than the Arch of Constantine, with gray and pink sandstone columns and marble ornaments, and with bold flowing Arabic inscriptions in a frieze on a white background. Akbar was very liberal and included among his mottoes one which he attributed to the founder of Christianity: "Said Jesus, on whom be peace: The world is a bridge; pass over it, but build not a house upon it. The world is but an hour; spend it in devotion, the rest is unseen."

Between the gateway and the mosque is a cloistered courtyard 500 feet square, containing a white marble tomb built to honor the body of the holy man who suggested Fattehpur-Sikri, so, Akbar believed, bringing to him his beloved son.

GOLCONDA ~

GOLCONDA, the city of the wondrous diamonds, was for three centuries the marvel of India. But the climate changed, the rains ceased, and nature succeeded in ousting the chiefs from that stronghold which they had considered impregnable.

Now it is a vast, silent ruin, reached by a parched road across a dreary plain piled with tumbled heaps of boulders. The Indians say that when God finished creation and these rocks were left over, He let them fall haphazard on the earth at Nizam.

The crested walls of Golconda, 30 feet high, with parapets and watch towers, inclose a whole mountain which has been cut into a series of bewildering ramparts and bastions, a superhuman task. For some strange reason the topmost stone was not cut into a buttress, but left round and unfinished, like a crude beast crouching on the summit.

The ponderous gates were spiked with iron to resist attack by elephants. Cisterns hollowed out of rocks collected water in case of siege. Winding subterranean passages for desperate flight led through the heart of the mountain and out to secret doors in the wall. There are many mosques for prayers and a kiosk near the summit where the sultan could watch for approaching armies.

Now those proud rulers lie in whitewashed mounds in the cemetery, and Golconda the supreme is abandoned to the desolation of endless drought.

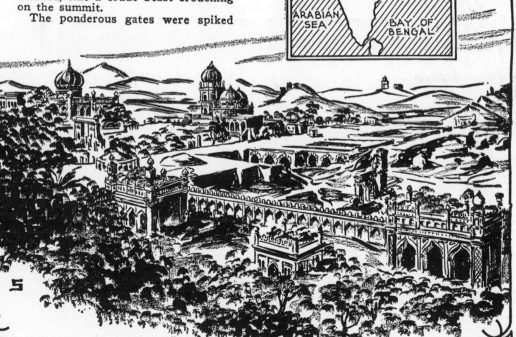

The GREAT BANYAN TREE, CALCUTTA

WOULD you believe that there is a single tree whose spread of branches covers three acres of ground? This tree, growing in the Botanical Gardens of Calcutta, India, is the Great Banyan, a species of fig, which under careful protection has grown into a vast mound of vegetation, which the gardeners say within a period of a few more years will cover an area of twenty acres.

The explanation of this amazing growth is that each branch of the parent tree develops roots which grow downward like stalactites, soon becoming new stems, until what was once a single trunk is now a veritable forest of trunks, hundreds of which have now attained the diameter of one of our large oaks. There are thousands of smaller stems, each of which is protected from harm by bar-

riers of bamboo, for the Calcuttans are determined to have the biggest tree in the world.

Because the banyan is such a rapidly growing tree, its wood is light and porous and of no commercial value. In time the parent stem will decay away, leaving the ever-expanding circle of younger trunks to carry on, as Milton describes them in "Paradise Lost":

"—the bended twigs take root, and daughters grow
About the mother tree, a pillard shade
High over-arched and echoing walks between."

The GREAT MOSQUE at DELHI

THE Jama Masjid, the Great Mosque at Delhi, is the second largest Mohammedan place of worship in the world, for it shelters a supreme treasure, the actual red hair of the beard of the Prophet. Planned by Shah Jehan in 1631 in honor of his daughter, it took 5000 men six years to complete it at the cost of many lakhs of rupees.

It is not perhaps the most beautiful mosque in India, but it is very imposing, as its minarets and domes rise from the plain about it, all a contrast of red sandstone and pure white marble. Large and impressive, it is raised on a platform with flights of steps leading up to the arcaded cloisters which surround it, and from which the corner minarets, 130 feet high, soar gracefully. The main courtyard, a broad granite plaza, 325 feet square, inlaid with marble, contains a huge tank for the ablutions of the faithful. Here, before the massive front portals which are never opened save to admit royal persons, a large open air pulpit stands, from which the throngs of bowed figures are addressed on the last day of Ramadan, the equivalent of the Christian Lent, when the daily fast from food, drink, and smoke is ended.

During the Indian Mutiny in 1857 the rebels fortified themselves against siege in the Great Mosque, but the damage from the fighting was perfectly repaired by the British Government and by munificent native rulers.

The GREAT TEMPLE at BUDDH GAYA

MORE than five centuries before the birth of Christ, Siddhartha Gautama made his "great renunciation." Leaving all that was dear to him, he fled into the jungles to solve the problems of human existence. He tried, first by meditation and later by self-torture, to find peace. After seven years of struggle he sat one day, a lonely recluse, beneath a bo tree (wild fig) at Gaya. Suddenly his mind became restful and cool. He discovered what he believed to be the cause and cure of suffering, and so became Buddha, the Enlightened One.

Asoka, a devout Indian emperor, built a shrine beside this famous bo tree, and later it was replaced by the larger temple, Buddh-Gaya, which now stands there. Quite different in architecture from other Indian temples, this great brick structure, 160 feet high, rises in nine diminishing stories like a pyramid, beautifully decorated. Within is a dark, cavelike chamber where torches burn continually before a large statue of Buddha. This was originally very simple, but in later centuries the Hindus claimed Buddha as the ninth incarnation of their god Vishnu and togged out the statue with tawdry prayer flags.

Around the temple are the remains of a sculptured stone railing, enclosing the sacred shrine and a widespreading bo tree, direct descendant of the one beneath which Buddha received his revelation 24 centuries ago.

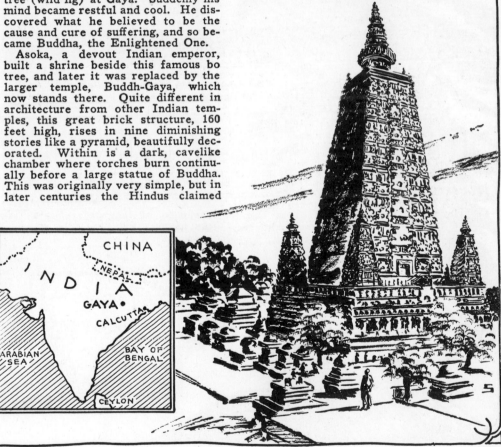

The GREAT WALL of CHINA

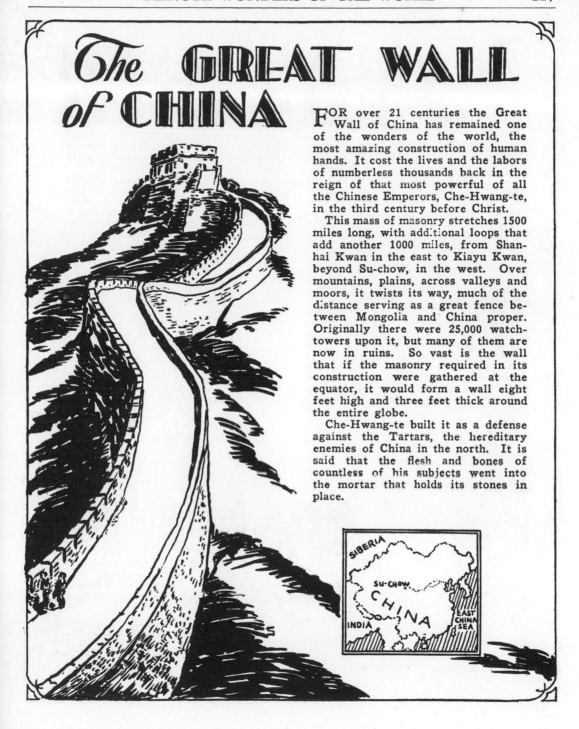

FOR over 21 centuries the Great Wall of China has remained one of the wonders of the world, the most amazing construction of human hands. It cost the lives and the labors of numberless thousands back in the reign of that most powerful of all the Chinese Emperors, Che-Hwang-te, in the third century before Christ.

This mass of masonry stretches 1500 miles long, with additional loops that add another 1000 miles, from Shan-hai Kwan in the east to Kiayu Kwan, beyond Su-chow, in the west. Over mountains, plains, across valleys and moors, it twists its way, much of the distance serving as a great fence between Mongolia and China proper. Originally there were 25,000 watch-towers upon it, but many of them are now in ruins. So vast is the wall that if the masonry required in its construction were gathered at the equator, it would form a wall eight feet high and three feet thick around the entire globe.

Che-Hwang-te built it as a defense against the Tartars, the hereditary enemies of China in the north. It is said that the flesh and bones of countless of his subjects went into the mortar that holds its stones in place.

The HANGING GARDENS of BABYLON

SINCE 600 B.C. men have praised the Hanging Gardens of Babylon as one of the Seven Wonders of the world—yet their accounts have been so glamorous that they were scarcely credited until excavations in 1903 confirmed the details.

It is supposed that Nebuchadnezzar designed these splendid gardens to delight his beautiful Median queen, Cyaxerxes. He placed them near his palace in the heart of Babylon. Stone is so scarce in that river valley that even a door socket was a prized gift; yet the imperious King ordered the entire structure, 350 feet high and covering a square mile, built of stone, even to the underground vaults where perishable foods were cooled.

The gardens were really an enormous series of fretted stone galleries, with tiers of elaborately carved arched and vaulted porches, each one with a thick layer of loam planted with gorgeous scented Oriental flowers and fruit-bearing trees. A hydraulic pump and complicated well system raised water to a reservoir on the roof, whence it flowed continually over the series of terraces, keeping them verdant even in the hot, dry air of Babylon. Lead under the soil prevented the dampness from seeping into the painted, frescoed chambers within, where Nebuchadnezzar and his court took their ease, cooled by the moist and fragrant airs wafted from the ever-watered gardens.

AN IMAGINATIVE RECONSTRUCTION

The KAABA at Mecca

MECCA was a holy place long before the days of Mohammed, for the Arabs believed that the black stone now built into the Kaaba, or "cube," which stood in its center, was given to Abraham by the archangel Gabriel. When the Prophet founded his religion, he took advantage of the established sanctity of Mecca and adopted the Kaaba as his own, merely destroying the heathen idols which the Arabs had ranged about it.

The Kaaba has been rebuilt several times, but without radical change. It is a rough windowless cube 40 feet each way, banded with silver. In its southeast angle is embedded the famous stone which thousands of pilgrims annually trek to Mecca to kiss. Every year the crude roughhewn outer walls are hidden in fresh rare and gorgeous brocades. The interior is of the richest marble, gold and silver.

Near by in the mosque plaza is the tomb of Mohammed. The prophet died in the house of his favorite, Ayesha, whose doorway led to the mosque courtyard. Since he had decreed that a prophet should be buried where he died, his simple tomb stands there, holding also the bodies of his successors, Abu Bekr and Caliph Omar.

Mecca is a mountain-locked and inaccessible town, and would be deserted, now that commerce no longer travels in caravans, were it not for the black stone of the Kaaba, which still draws thousands of the devout every year to its sacred plaza.

The LION PALACE on the ROCK

A SOLITARY giant boss of rock lifts abruptly 400 feet above the jungle in the heart of Ceylon. This was the natural fortress to which Kasyapa fled in 511 A.D., after starving his father to death and stealing the Sacred Tooth, sign of royal power, from his elder brother, Moggallana.

Narrow staircases wound miraculously up the steep sides of the cliff, starting from between the paws of a great lion. On the summit plateau are the ruins of an elaborate Oriental palace, an acre of labyrinths of passages, galleries, and room foundations of well-burned brick, the wooden superstructure having long since disintegrated. A 30-yard-square cistern cut from a boulder and surrounded by smaller pools evidently caught a water supply from the monsoon rains. Near the edge of the cliff, overlooking the green sea of trees far below, is an impressive throne of red gneiss from which Kasyapa ruled.

Innumerable native huts for slaves clustered at the base of the castle rock. These Sinhalese were advanced in cultural development, for there are remarkable frescoes of court scenes in faded color still on the rocky walls.

Here Kasyapa ruled in splendor and fear for eighteen years. Then, somehow, he was enticed out of his stronghold to meet his brother in mortal combat. He fell, and Moggallana moved the court back to the capital city, abandoning Sigiri, the Lion Palace, to the monsoon and the jungle.

LION ROCK

SPIRAL STAIRWAY
OF THE FORTRESS ROCK

The MAUSOLEUM at HALICARNASSUS

IN THE fourth century B.C. a noble prince, Mausolus, ruled a Persian satrapy in Halicarnassus, now Budrum. When he died, his heartbroken Queen Artemisia resolved to erect for him the most splendid tomb ever known. The renowned Greek architects, Satyros and Pythios, and the sculptor Scopas set to work. In two years the widow died, consumed with grief, but the structure was completed, to become one of the Seven Wonders of the World.

It was a magnificent marble building, 140 feet high, with a solid lower story surmounted by an Ionic colonnade bearing a pyramid topped by a majestic four-horse chariot bearing the King and Queen. This beautifully proportioned tomb rose from a great rectangular courtyard walled with golden white marble. The long flight of steps leading to it was guarded by a series of lifelike lions, all expressing power, balance, and majesty. Three carved colored friezes encircled the building, one depicting a battle between Greeks and Amazons, the second, a chariot race, and the third, Greeks and Centaurs.

In 1402 the Knights of St. John seized Halicarnassus and destroyed the sepulchre. About 1850 the Sultan of Turkey permitted the removal of the fragments to the British Museum. There one may view all that remains of that tomb which was so wonderful that all elaborate sepulchres since have been called mausoleums.

AN IMAGINATIVE RECONSTRUCTION

MESHED, the holy shrine of Persia

MESHED, the capital of Persian Khorasan, has ever been attacked and besieged throughout its long history, for it holds the frontier. Its fame, however, is due not to its military career, but to its being the burial place of Imam Reza, the eighth of the twelve prophets whom the Shia sect of Mohammedans reverence next to Mohammed himself. This saint was buried there in the ninth century A.D. According to legend, he died of poison treacherously given him by a jealous caliph, and so Meshed (Martyrdom) was named to commemorate his death, and a magnificent mosque was built there in his honor. As it is considered a virtue to be buried near to such a saint, the town is full of cemeteries.

It possesses a feature unique in the Orient, a main street one and three-fourths miles long actually straight, and at the end of this approach the golden domes and minarets of the mosque rise in great beauty over the small squat buildings of the city.

The mosque stands in a quadrangle 150 paces square, with rows of alcoves on three sides and gigantic archways for entrances. Over the west archway is a cage to which the muezzin ascends to give the call to prayer. The marble tomb of the Imam is surrounded by silver railings with knobs of gold, and is accounted most beautiful; but it is rarely seen, for because of its sanctity unbelievers are not allowed to go into or to gaze at the interior of the famous mosque.

The MING TOMBS near Peking ~

Arch of Five Spears-one of the entrance gates to Ming Tombs.

(Peiping) PEKING •
CHINESE REPUBLIC

THE famous Ming Tombs and the grotesque stone figures that guard them are relics of the most romantic Chinese period, the Ming or "Bright" Dynasty, a powerful house founded in 1366 by the son of a Nanking laborer.

The great Kublai Khan, mighty Mongol, consolidated half of Asia under Chinese rule, but his weak successors allowed the empire to dwindle, until 73 years later there was great dissatisfaction with his house.

In the meantime a farm boy, Choo, too delicate for hard work, had been placed in a monastery to become a "bonze." He did not aspire to the priesthood, however, and left to join the army, where he rose rapidly. After marrying a rich widow and becoming still more ambitious, he headed a successful insurrection and led all the dissatisfied in a rebel army which seized the Imperial throne. He and his descendants then ruled for 300 years.

A wide treeless plain 40 miles north of Peking was set aside for their tombs. A magnificent gateway of white marble and red tile, with five openings, leads to a mile-long avenue guarded by colossal stone figures of weird men and beasts. The thirteen tombs themselves are merely huge mounds of earth, with apparently no entrances, each with a 20-foot crenellated retaining wall around the half-mile circuit of its base. There is nothing to mark the exact resting spot of these emperors whose dynasty started with the farm boy Choo.

Gigantic monuments line the road to the tombs of the Ming Emperors of China.

They form an avenue two miles long.

MOUNT EVEREST-
SECOND PEAK FROM
THE LEFT - FROM
A PHOTOGRAPH TAKEN
90 MILES AWAY.

MOUNT EVEREST

THE highest mountain on the globe is yet to be conquered by man, though men in airplanes have recently skimmed through the clouds above it and looked down upon the goal they could not reach on foot. Mount Everest, towering 29,000 feet (5½ miles) into the sky, between Nepal and Tibet in the Himalaya range, was named for Sir George Everest, Surveyor-general of India, who first fixed its position and altitude by trigonometrical observation in 1841.

Snow-covered all the year round, Mount Everest with its steep slopes has defied the many attempts to reach its summit. By the use of oxygen (the air at this height is too rarefied to sustain life) one expedition recently got to within 1500 feet of the top before it had to turn back.

Until 1904 when Sir Francis Younghusband entered Tibet, no white man had ever gazed upon this great pile of rock and snow except from the direction of India, where a complete view is obscured by another mountain, which is sometimes confused with Everest. Even up to 1921 no white man had been within 50 miles of its base. It is only a matter of time, however, when this last stronghold of nature will have been conquered by some bold explorer in the face of its intense cold, its sudden avalanches, and its towering height.

At its base stands a monument erected to all of those who have perished so far in the attempt to reach the bleak crest 5½ miles above it.

The entrance to the Toshogu-Shrine

NIKKO, the Glory of Japan~

A JAPANESE proverb says: "Do not use the word magnificent until you have seen Nikko!" Truly, it is very beautiful, for to this mountain spot with great forest trees and tumbling cascades, a triumph of Nature, was added a collection of superb shrines and mausolea when Japanese wood carving and painting was at its height in the seventeenth century. The great Shogun Ieyasu, founder of the Tokugawa Dynasty, and his famous grandson Iemitsu were responsible for choosing the site.

Nikko is approached through a 20-mile avenue of huge cryptomerias, whose sombre foliage sheds a dim cathedral light over the road. The rapid Daiya-gawa is crossed by a wide bridge, 40 yards from which is the red-lacquered Mihashi, the Sacred Bridge, which only the mikado may traverse.

The whole mountain side is forested with a grove of ancient trees, and in occasional clearings the temples are clustered, all scarlet and gold, like beautiful gems in their dark green setting. These gorgeously carved buildings are really enormous, but overshadowed by the great trees, they seem like dainty miniatures, each one a charming jewel of light.

The tombs of the mighty Shoguns, however, are severely simple, of plain green bronze, in humble contrast to the handsome luxuriance of their tributes to the gods.

PAGAN'S 10,000 TEMPLES

PAGAN was once a lavishly beautiful city, stretching for 25 miles along the Irrawaddy, gleaming with 10,000 gorgeous temples clustered about by myriads of the little mat huts of the Burmese. Now only a handful of natives drive their bullock carts listlessly through the weedy streets, and the tropic jungle is relentlessly swallowing the city, for Pagan has been deserted for 700 years.

It was founded in A.D. 847, and in A.D. 1050 Arrawrata brought an immense population there to build the world's most splendid Oriental shrines to Buddha. So the sacred city flourished for 200 years. Then its King, Nara-thi-ha-pati, made the fatal mistake of killing ten Chinese emissaries. The Emperor of China with a vast army descended on Pagan, sacked it, annihilated its people, and left it an empty ruin.

Some of its 10,000 temples which escaped destruction are among the most beautiful in the world. The Ananda, or Endless, is the largest, a tremendous pile of brick, yet exquisitely light and delicate in its carvings and filigree and pinnacles. Its main dome is seven stories high, intricately ornamented. Each of its four projecting wings contains a 30-foot statue of Buddha each in a different incarnation. Thousands of niches in the tiled walls hold carved groups depicting the life of Buddha. Grotesque lionlike creatures forever stand guard by the entrances to this fantastic temple, whose grandeur now rises in melancholy splendor from the relentless jungle closing in around it.

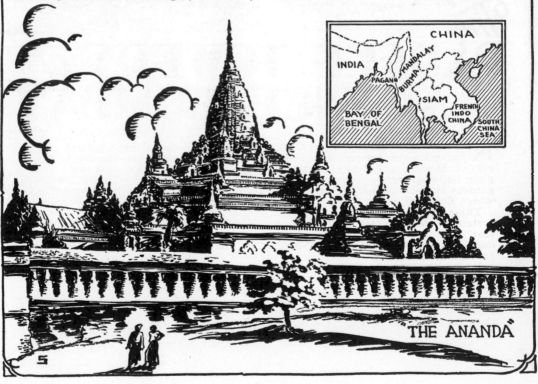

"THE ANANDA"

The PARSEE TOWERS of SILENCE, BOMBAY

NEAR Bombay on a great hill the Parsees have erected five Towers of Silence, gray-white, severely plain buildings set in gloomy cypress gardens and surrounded by high walls where flocks of vultures sit, waiting.

These are part of the strange burial system of the Parsees, who believe that in death rich and poor meet as one, and that Earth, Fire, and Water prevent all pollution.

Four carriers of the dead bear each corpse to the Tower entrance, followed by the mourners and two bearded men. These are the only ones permitted to enter. They place the naked dead on a center platform, and within a few moments the cloud of vultures have picked the bones, which remain to bleach and dry. Then the carriers of the dead with tongs in gloved hands cast them into a deep well, through which rainwater constantly seeps, crumbling them to dust, and passing on through charcoal beds to the sea.

After the ceremony the bearded men purify themselves by bathing in a sacred pool, while the mourners link their clothes together in a fashion which has a mystic meaning.

The torrential rains, hot suns, keen winds, and hunger of the vultures make this weird system more sanitary than it sounds. So complete is the destruction of the corpses that in 40 years only five feet of sediment has collected in the sacred well.

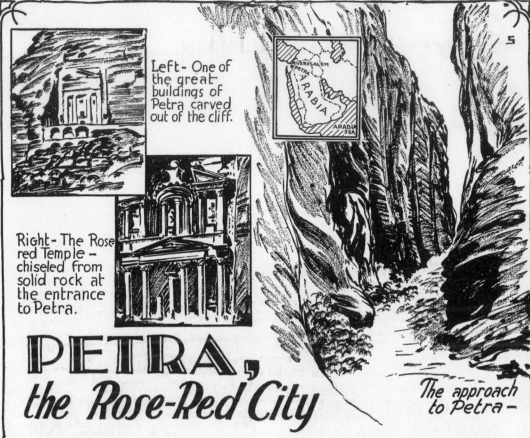

Left- One of the great buildings of Petra carved out of the cliff.

Right- The Rose red Temple – chiseled from solid rock at the entrance to Petra.

PETRA, the Rose-Red City

The approach to Petra –

WHEN the traffic between the Eastern and Western worlds filed in caravans over the Arabian desert, travelers told vague tales of a mysterious race who held the mountains between the Dead and the Red Seas. There was but one pass through this hill kingdom, a tortuous gorge 1200 feet deep, closed in by towering walls of rose-red sandstone. Here one man could repulse an army, and here it was that the lean, hawk-faced Rockmen exacted tribute, becoming all-powerful and wealthy. Until 1807, Petra, their beautiful mountain city, was merely a legend, and today few have seen its ruins; but those who have were amply repaid.

It is built on a mountain side whose crags are rose-red, lilac, and golden yellow. A hill, inaccessible save from one side, overshadows it, topped by the Place of Sacrifice with altar and blood basin. Ancient Petra was carved out of these many-hued cliffs; and layers of tombs rise beside the dwellings, the temples, and the open theatre.

The city was ornate and beautiful, its architecture reflecting many influences: Egyptian pylons, Persian sculpture, Greek ornaments, Syrian arches, and last, Roman columns and circular shields. For the Emperor Trajan in 106 finally reduced proud Petra to a Roman province, beginning its decline, until now the iridescent city is merely a haunt for a handful of Arab robbers.

The PORCELAIN PAGODA

CHINESE REPUBLIC NANKING

PACIFIC OCEAN

ONE of the most beautiful and fantastic shrines of the Orient was the Porcelain Pagoda outside of Nanking. This nine-story tower, 200 feet high, with its little green-tiled roofs and cornices hung with bells, and its tall spire topped with a golden ball, was made of brick by the Buddhists and completely overlaid with porcelain.

The site has been sacred since 371 A.D., when a three-story pagoda, part of the Monastery of Celestial Felicity, was built there to shelter a precious relic. About 1430 the Great Yungloh of the Ming Dynasty labored to build it higher and overlay it according to a plate pattern in his palace, for porcelain was then unbelievably precious.

At its peak a dragon head was hung by eight iron chains, and 72 bells, suspended from it, tinkled in the breeze. Eighty more bells hung from the upturned corners of the roofs. The tower was octagonal and lighted by 128 oil lamps. At the top were deposited tea, gold, silver, yellow silk, sacred religious volumes, and pearls for illuminating the night and for warding off the evils of water, fire, wind, and dust.

Evidently the pearl for warding off evil was not very efficacious, for later a third of the pagoda was destroyed by lightning. Finally, in 1853 this unusual shrine with its lustrous porcelain walls was destroyed by the Taipings.

The POTALA PALACE, LHASA

WHEN Younghusband's expedition, in 1904, reached the gates of Lhasa, perched two miles above sea level in the mountains of Tibet, no living white man had set eyes upon this forbidden city. This strange isolation is not because of its inaccessibility, however, but because the lamas, or priests, antagonistic to any form of enlightenment, have kept Lhasa the last stronghold of mediævalism.

Above the plain, where the squalid city lies, three huge monasteries crown the surrounding hills, Sera, Gaden, and De-bung, the latter housing over 8000 lamas. But dwarfing all these, and rising tier upon tier upon the hillside, the palace of Dalai Lama, the Potala, dominates the city.

Three hundred feet above the plain, like the façade of a modern dam, this huge curtain of stone pierced by countless windows thrusts its massive bulk above the green slope up which the zig-zagging staircases climb. The buttresses and wings, 900 feet across, are whitewashed a gleaming white. Here live the crimson-clad under-priests. But the great central building, where dwells the Dalai, himself, is tinted a rich red-crimson, and from its roof, hiding the central recess, stretches a brown yak-hair curtain, 80 feet in length and 25 feet across. Glittering roofs of gold against the blue of the sky, the brilliant white and crimson of the walls, the green of the hillside—few of us will ever behold this ancient palace in the fastnesses of the Himalayas, but there it stands, one of the most imposing religious buildings in all the world!

The ROCK of BEHISTUN

NEAR an old caravan road leading down to Babylon, a towering rocky headland rises 4000 feet above the Persian plain. On the face of this mighty and enduring rock Darius, King of Kings, in 500 B.C. ordered the history of his reign carved—so miraculously engraved on the inaccessible sheer precipice that no enemy could obliterate it. He wanted his story told in three languages, Persian, Susian, and Babylonian, that all passing travelers might understand. He ordered pictures drawn, so that even illiterates might learn of his valor. So, though we cannot fathom how, the history of Darius was carved in four ways on the face of a cliff where it seems that even a lizard could not have clung.

But as ages passed, the key to the cuneiform characters was forgotten and the story could no longer be deciphered. In 1835 a young English soldier, Henry Rawlinson, was stationed in that province. He had a flair for language and adventure, and he risked his life to scale the rock and copy the inscriptions. Guessing that the four accounts described the same events, he translated first the Persian and later the Susian and Babylonian versions, his work giving a key which has been the basis ever since for deciphering ancient cuneiform inscriptions throughout the world, unlocking secrets which have long baffled archæologists and historians.

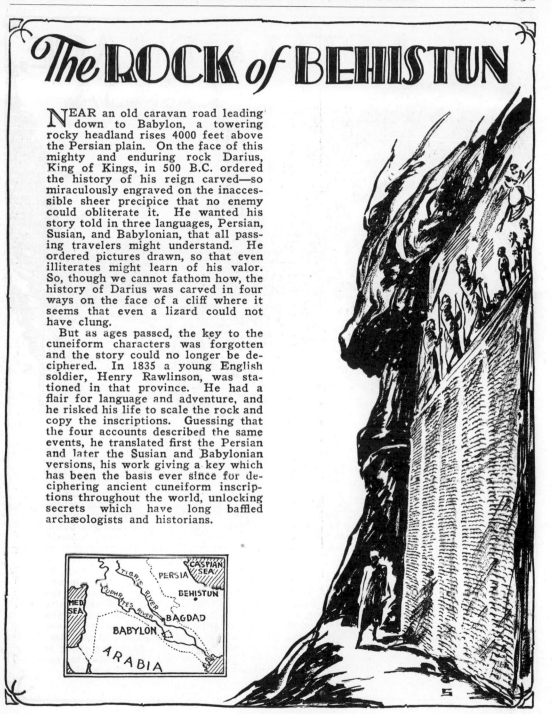

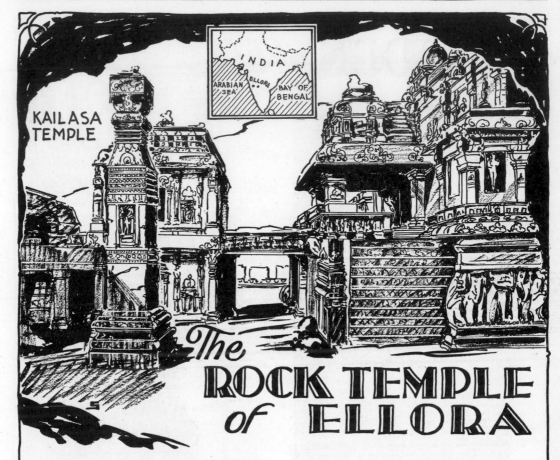

KAILASA TEMPLE

INDIA

ARABIAN SEA · ELLORA · BAY OF BENGAL

The ROCK TEMPLE of ELLORA

IN 757 A.D. Krishna I overtnrew his enemies and established his dynasty. As a fitting tribute to his god Siva, he designed Kailasa, "the abode of the gods," a vast stone Hindu temple at Ellora in South India, the finest monolith in the world, for it is carved out of the solid rock of a mountain. He chose a site where great cliffs rise in a wall above a lovely valley, sending his masons to the plateau above to mark out a space 280 by 160 feet. Then by digging trenches 150 feet deep they laboriously detached this huge block and carved it into an exquisite temple with spiral staircases, bridges, colonnades, and galleries without end. What years of toil it took to turn this mountain rock into an ornate temple, how many thousands of chisels picked out its sculptures, what armies of elephants were required to cart away the débris, we can only guess.

Now, after eleven centuries, it is still incomparably beautiful and majestic. The chief shrine is a pagoda 96 feet high, apparently borne on the backs of hundreds of elephants standing side by side around its base.

The holiest chamber is small and dark, to symbolize the mystery of Siva, but completely carved with symbolic motifs. Ellora is a sacred spot and abounds in many religious shrines, but Kailasa overshadows them all with its size and grandeur.

The RUINS of PERSEPOLIS

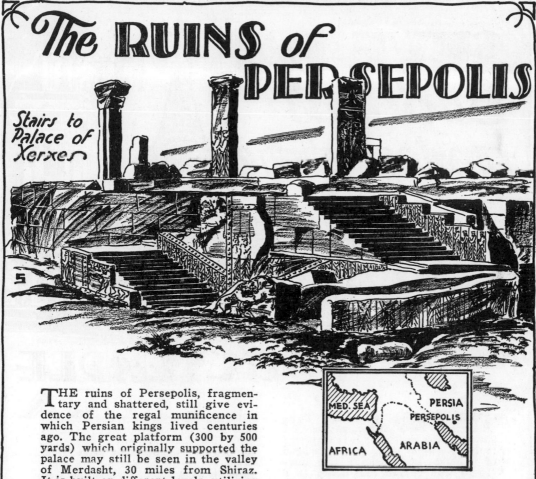

Stairs to Palace of Xerxes

THE ruins of Persepolis, fragmentary and shattered, still give evidence of the regal munificence in which Persian kings lived centuries ago. The great platform (300 by 500 yards) which originally supported the palace may still be seen in the valley of Merdasht, 30 miles from Shiraz. It is built on different levels, utilizing the natural contours of the ground and leads to a site from which the edifice dominated the countryside.

The famous great staircase is there, a long, gradual ascent to the magnificent porch of Xerxes, flanked by the heavy piers with powerful bas-reliefs of winged bulls eighteen feet high. It bears this inscription of Xerxes: "By the grace of Ormuzd I have made this portal!," and describes other buildings of the group as being the work of himself and of his father, Darius. These gorgeous halls were solely for royal, not religious, use. The roof of the audience chamber of Xerxes was up-held by 72 columns 67 feet high with bull heads for capitals. The central room covered 60,000 feet.

The Palace of Darius is almost obliterated now, for its walls of sun-baked brick have disintegrated. This was the palace which, according to Diodorus, Alexander the Great burned, pretending to be in a drunken frolic, but really avenging the destruction of the Temple of Athens by Xerxes. In 1878, when it was excavated, the ashes of its cedar roof still lay thick on the paved floor, mute testimony to the conqueror's act of reprisal 2200 years ago.

SHWE DAGON, *Buddha's greatest shrine*

THE beautiful glittering Shwe Dagon is the most famous Buddhist shrine in the world, for it is supposed to shelter eight hairs from the head of Buddha, bestowed on two merchants who offered him honey in a forest in 586 B.C.

This pagoda rises on the outskirts of Rangoon in Burma, and its golden dome can be seen flashing 30 miles away. It was originally only 27 feet high, but was constantly added to, until in 1564 it reached its present height of 370 feet. A colony of smaller pagodas, shrines, and bazaars clusters about its feet. One passes these and mounts between leogryphs and fantastic fabulous animals up long flights of steps covered with teak roofs carved into minarets and turrets, until one comes out upon a great platform 900 by 685 feet. From its center the huge bell-shaped pagoda rises, covered with solid gold, its peak topped by a hti or "umbrella" incrusted with jewels and tinkling with innumerable little silver bells.

About 1500 small shrines cling to the edges of the platform, a haphazard array representing gifts from many nations, some decaying, others shining new, for the Buddhist is rewarded not for preserving but for building temples. Many are tawdry and crude with cheap colored glass and atrocious woodwork, but others are beautiful with master carving of the nats or fairies who protect Buddhists and with alabaster scenes of the saint's life. Their multiplicity emphasizes the serenity of the old pagoda raising its burnished dome high above the clamor and confusion below.

The TAJ MAHAL

THE Taj Mahal has been accounted the most perfect building in the world, and its beauty and its romantic history have attracted travellers since the seventeenth century. It is the unique tribute from the Emperor Shah Jehan to his wife Mumtazi Mahal, the Chosen of the Palace. Theirs is one of the famous love stories of the world, especially since at that time in India woman was considered merely a plaything, and Shah Jehan followed a faith which still denies her a soul.

When she died after fourteen years of ideal companionship, the grief-stricken Emperor determined to erect such a tomb for her as the world had never seen. He summoned Ustad-Isa, a cunning architect, French jewelers, and Italian painters. Under their direction 20,000 men labored for seven-teen years to complete the memorial.

Certainly it is exquisite, of whitest marble, with its pure dome gleaming against the blue sky of India and mir-rored in the long pool that stretches before it. Minarets rising a little apart from the main structure impart grace and delicacy.

The interior is rich in mosaics and grillwork, the masterpiece being the jewelled trellis which surrounds the elaborate sarcophagi. The tomb of Mumtazi lies directly beneath the dome in the place of honor, while that of Shah Jehan is near by at one side. These are empty, according to Eastern custom, the actual bodies being laid in the crypt below, side by side, in unadorned simplicity beneath the Taj Mahal whose magnificence tells of a wonderful devotion.

The TEMPLE of 33,333 GODS

SAN-JU-SAN-GEN-DO at Kyoto is the longest temple in Japan. It is used as the official test for archers, since only the most skillful can send an arrow its full length of 389 feet.

It is more famous, however, because it contains no less than 33,333 gods, all slightly differing figures of Kwannon, the Thousand-handed Goddess of Mercy. It was begun in 1132 A.D. by Emperor Toba with 1001 images; but in 1266 the Emperor Kameyama rebuilt it, filling it from end to end with carved wooden statues, gold-lacquered, a dazzling and bright array.

The 1000 main figures are five feet high, surrounded by tier on tier of lesser images, no two identical. There is infinite variety in the placing of the hands, of the clothes, and of the ornaments. None has less than a dozen hands.

The central figure, surrounded by the Bushu, or Eight and Twenty Followers, is a great Kwannon with a skull embedded in its head. The Emperor Go-Shirakawa, troubled with persistent headaches, learned in a dream that a pious monk's skull was lying untended in a river bed near the roots of a swaying willow. He rescued this relic and set it in the Sacred Head of Kwannon, so being relieved of his suffering. Now it forms part of that holiest of all the statues in the fantastic and elaborate temple of 33,333 gods.

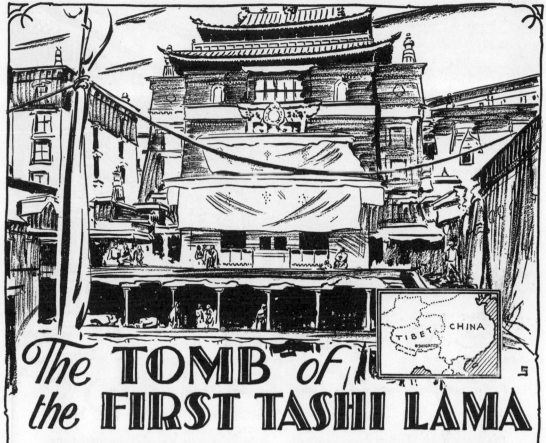

The TOMB of the FIRST TASHI LAMA

SECOND only to the Dalai Lama of Lhasa, who is so sacred that anyone who sees him loses his sight, the Tashi Lama is the head of the Buddhist faith, to which it is said one-third of the world owes allegiance. His headquarters are at Shigatse, Tibet, and close by is the most beautiful lamasery in the world, called Tashi Lhumpo. Here, in numerous gorgeous temples and unbelievably filthy dwellings, 4500 lamas spend their lives guarding five golden tombs of the former Tashi Lamas.

The tomb of the first is the most lavishly decorated. Like the others, its gilded roof rises high over the two and three stories of the monastery near by, and contains the elaborate sarcophagus, a golden jewelled cube 25 feet square, with a cover like a Chinese roof hung with silks and tapestries. Designs worked in matched turquoises and precious stones embroider it. Even the polished concrete of the floor is studded with turquoises. Along the ridges of the tomb are cloisonné vases and golden bowls holding lighted tapers. In a niche at the summit sits a figure of the dead Tashi Lama, his neck festooned with pearls, for in death he is permitted the ornaments forbidden during his life.

Strangely enough, among the jewels of the solid gold tomb hang five colored glass Christmas tree ornaments, considered great prizes by the monks, who live out their long, quiet, and sequestered lives guarding this gorgeous sepulchre.

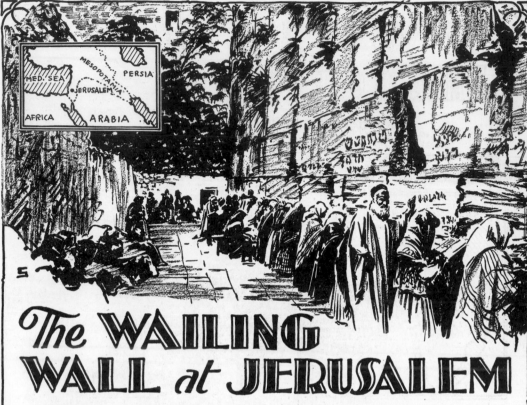

The WAILING WALL at JERUSALEM

THE "Wailing Place of the Jews" is the long wall which once fortified the Haram or "Noble Sanctuary" of the great temple at Jerusalem. Here it is that Jews of all ages and from all countries stop to bewail the lost splendor of their ancient capital and the desecration of the temple. The wall is 150 feet long and 56 feet high, composed of immense blocks of stone, some measuring 16 feet in length. The Palestine architects well understood how to use these gigantic blocks, for they stand solidly in place today, in spite of the centuries since Solomon's builders placed them there. It is believed that each of these stones was prepared and fitted at the quarries for its exact position in the wall.

The group of devout Jews who gather at all times to wail are a strange sight. The women often actually weep; the men usually read from the Scriptures or mutter prayers, occasionally rubbing their cheeks against the rough blocks or perhaps kissing them until many of the stones have become smooth and polished from the years of friction. Swarming about is the motley crowd of beggars common to all Eastern cities, diseased and maimed, filthy and ragged. But even these creatures and the strangeness of the wailing cannot make one forget the essential pathos of the scene, for this solid gray stone rampart is all that remains of the national home of that race which is now scattered to the ends of the earth.

The WALLS of JERICHO

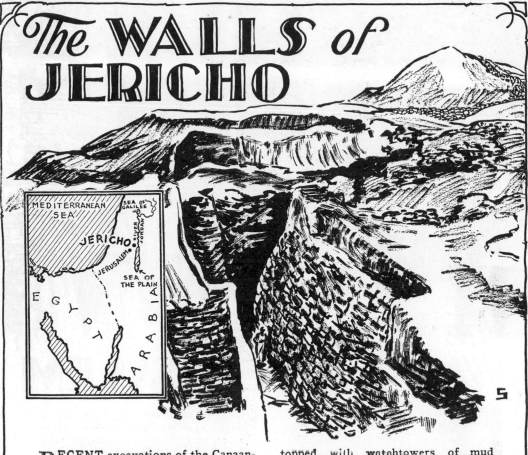

RECENT excavations of the Canaan-itish fortress of Jericho show how remarkable it was that Joshua and his army could conquer it, and justify the inclusion of that victory in the Bible as one of the major feats of the Children of Israel.

Until 1907 ancient Jericho was merely a vast oval mound called Tell Es-Sultan, 1½ miles from modern Jericho, 180 yards long, rising 50 feet above the plain about it, and topped by smaller mounds. Professor Sellin excavated this from the sand which had covered it for centuries and remarkably preserved it, and discovered the Jericho which Joshua captured.

The outer walls, eight feet thick at the base, were of great stone blocks set on a natural stone foundation, topped with watchtowers of mud brick. The spaces in the center of the wall between the blocks were filled with smaller stones to defy besiegers' weapons. The masonry is similar to that found at Troy and suggests the same methods, those of the seventeenth to fourteenth centuries B.C.

The walls enclosed a citadel, itself doubly walled and towered, which sheltered a veritable rabbit warren of small dwellings with a narrow street winding among them.

These strong battlements rose solidly from the surrounding barren plains. How impregnable they must have looked to the little army of Joshua, approaching on foot over the open flats to attack with nothing to shelter or screen their movements!

The WAT PHRA KEO, Bangkok

The Emerald Buddha and the King's Wat where he sits

THE great temple of Phra Keo was started in 1785 A.D. by King Chulalok, founder of the present dynasty, in honor of the Emerald Buddha. This very beautiful green jade figure was discovered at Kiang Hai in 1436 A.D. and is now enshrined in the Obosot and carefully tended, being dressed in a variety of gold-trimmed costumes, according to the time of year.

King Chulalonkorn in 1879 vowed to finish the temple, which had been left incomplete, and he defrayed the expense from his private purse. His many relatives lent their aid, one re laying the marble courtyard, a second renewing the stone inscriptions, a third repairing the brass paving, a fourth restoring the pearl inlaid work, and a fifth mending the ceilings.

Now it is a most beautiful and elaborate group of buildings, enclosed by frescoed walls, the gates guarded, as in all Siamese temples, by grotesque and fantastic figures of men and beasts to frighten away evil spirits. The courtyards abound in countless small gilded pagodas, by the building of which individuals hope to attain eternal merit. The gorgeously inlaid Phra Marodop in the form of a cross rises in the exact center of them all. Here also every half year is celebrated the cermony of the drinking of the water of allegiance, the princes pledging fealty to the king in water sanctified by the priests of Wat Phra Keo.

WAT PO, Bangkok

One of the sixteen gateways

CLOSE to the walls of the royal palace in picturesque Bangkok, capital of Siam, is Wat Po, the largest of the countless temple monasteries in that Buddhist kingdom. It is a widespread cluster of minarets and prachedi, or votive spires, topped by ringed masts representing the umbrellas-of-honor with which pious Indians used to crown their relic mounds. A high wall with carved gates guarded by grotesque and horrible figures surrounds gardens full of dwarfed and stunted trees of Chinese influence, of monstrous granite statues, and of ponds where the priests tend the sacred crocodiles.

The great Wat has a mouldy air of decay about it now, but it is still visited by many pilgrims, for it contains the tremendous reclining figure of Buddha, 175 feet long, called the Dying Buddha. This statue shows the saint lying on one side. It is built of brick, covered with cement and lacquer and such heavy gold leaf that for years it was supposed to be of solid gold. The soles of the feet, each five yards long, are inlaid with mother-of-pearl.

In a near-by cloister there are whole rows of Buddha figures, each crowned with the Sirot, or "glory." This is their halo—not round, but like a curiously pointed cranium with refulgent hair rising flamelike from the head, signifying the spiritual strivings of the soul.

The WHITE PALACE at Ctesiphon

CTESIPHON, downstream from Bagdad at a bend in the Tigris, was for centuries before the birth of Christ the winter capital of the Parthians, finally growing from a village into a wealthy city. In 531 A.D. a great Sassanian prince, Chosroes I, came to the throne, and built the famous White Palace, laying out gardens and hunting parks, and assembling treasures which sound like the Arabian Nights: a gold horse with emerald teeth, ruby-studded neck, silver saddle, and gold trappings; a silver camel with a golden foal; a banqueting carpet 70 cubits long by 60 broad, of gold decorated with jewels; a king's throne of gold.

But this glory was short-lived, for Chosroes was a Christian, and the Moslems considered Ctesiphon fair booty. The plains about it were void of natural fortifications. The ruthless Saad, the Moslem leader, easily sacked the rich city, getting so much plunder that he consecrated the White Palace as a place of thanksgiving.

Then, after a few years, the Arabs found the spot unhealthy and abandoned it, carrying away as much as possible, and reducing beautiful Ctesiphon to a rubbish heap. However, parts of the solid masonry of the palace withstood their pickaxes, and now the great vault of its audience chamber, always open to the air on one side, with its blue star-spangled ceiling, still stands in the desert—this great arch the only survival of a once luxurious empire.

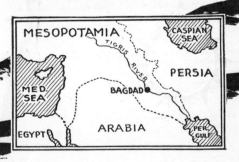

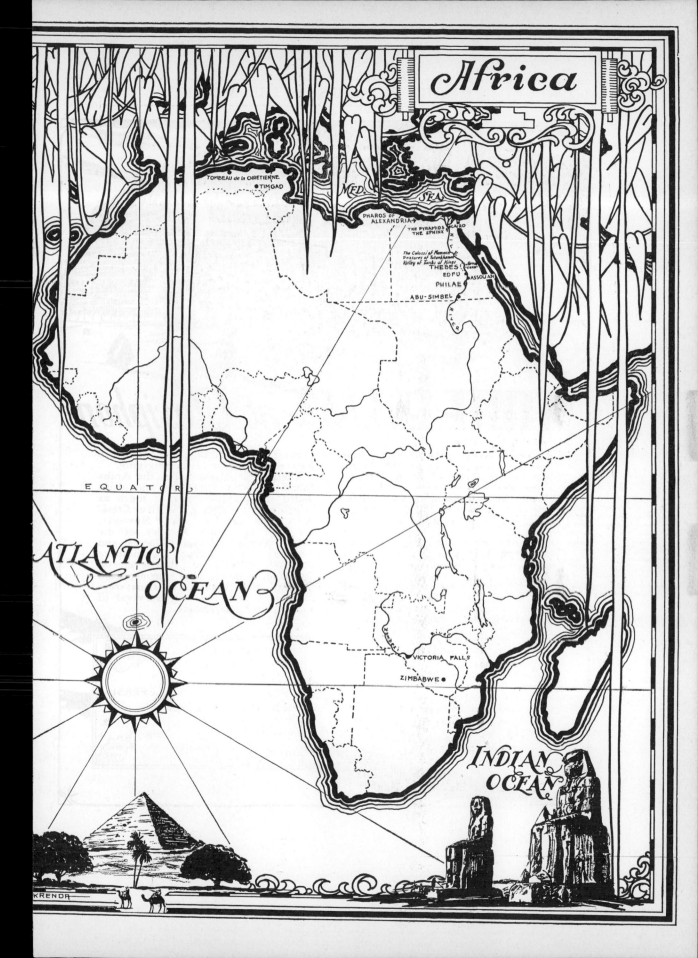

The ASSOUAN DAM

ASSOUAN is the most picturesque spot in upper Egypt, for here the Nile flows swiftly with rapids and cataracts between high rocky mountains covered with warm golden sand. This locality provided the granite for the sarcophagi and obelisks of the ancient Pharaohs, and abounds in quarries, tombs, and beautiful ruins. It was the logical place for a reservoir which might save Egypt from its frequent fatal droughts, but only after long struggles with the antiquarians did engineers succeed in damming the Nile and flooding that valley, including thousands of historical remains and the Island of Philae with its cluster of pyloned temples and halls.

The Assouan Dam is a colossal barrier of granite stretching across the river from mountain to mountain and forming behind it a vast lake with over 1,000,000,000 cubic yards of water. So great is its surface that evaporation alone carries off 1,000,000 cubic yards of water every 24 hours. The wall of the dam is pierced with 180 enormous sluices through which the water rushes thunderously, relieving pressure on the barrier.

A strange feature is that the flooding of Philae, which was expected to ruin the old temples, has really preserved them, hardening and resetting their crumbling sandstone foundations. Now for five months of the year at low water they stand out in all their glory, while the lake about them, held by the Assouan Dam, has saved Egypt from famine many times.

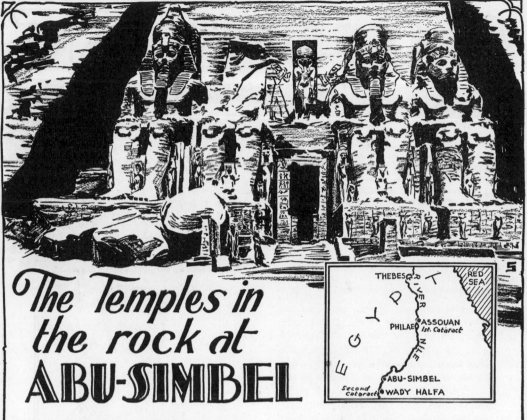

The Temples in the rock at ABU-SIMBEL

THERE is a rocky cliff at Abu-Simbel about which the Nile bends. Here a temple was carved out of the solid bank to face due east, dedicated to Ra-Harmakhis, the Rising Sun.

Four colossal statues seated in calm contemplation guard the entrance. They represent Pharaoh Rameses II on his throne in full regalia, wearing the striped linen headdress worn only by kings, the double diadem of Egypt, and the royal serpent on his brow. Clustered about the feet are the queen and her daughters, dwarfed by the tremendous proportions of the main figures.

Within the temple are dim, long, shadowy corridors stretching between lofty pillars. The inner shrine is so placed that at sunrise each morning a shaft of light passes between the colossal statues and illumines it with a temporary dazzling brilliance.

The walls of the Great Hall picture the Battle of Kadesh, the spectacular defeat of the Hittites by Rameses II. The Pharaoh found himself trapped, his army about to be annihilated. He called upon the god Ammon who heartened his men so that they turned fiercely against the enemy, driving them into the river, where their chariots were overturned and they were drowned by hundreds.

This dramatic confusion is not, however, the dominant feature of the temple. Instead, the memory that one carries away is of the unearthly, imperturbable colossi, eternally facing the sunrise by the great entrance.

The COLOSSI of MEMNON

INSCRUTABLE and gigantic, the Colossi of "Memnon" face the sunrise from their commanding position on the west bank of the Nile at Thebes, guarding the silent tombs of the pharaohs. They were carved 3000 years ago for Amenhotep III, quarried from a red mountain perhaps at Edfu, and brought along the Nile in light, specially constructed ships. They were among the first statues to be used instead of obelisks for monuments, and were the wonder of the times. Their architect prophesied: "They will last as long as heaven."

Actually they were portraits of Amenhotep III and his consort Tiyi—but the Greeks and Romans attributed them, with the architectural wonders round about, to the mythical Memnon, who fell at Troy—hence their name.

Originally, when surmounted by the tiara of united Egypt, they were 70 feet high. An earthquake broke one about 27 A.D. and at sunrise there-after it was said to emit a plaintive musical lament which travellers came miles to hear. Modern science explains this as the probable action of warm sun on cold stone. But Septimus Severus about 200 A.D. repaired it crudely with layers of sandstone blocks, and now its cry is silenced.

The thrones are ornamented with family portraits and hieroglyphs.

The Colossi were placed there to flank a great pylon entrance to a temple shrine which has long since disappeared, leaving them alone in their scarred, impressive grandeur.

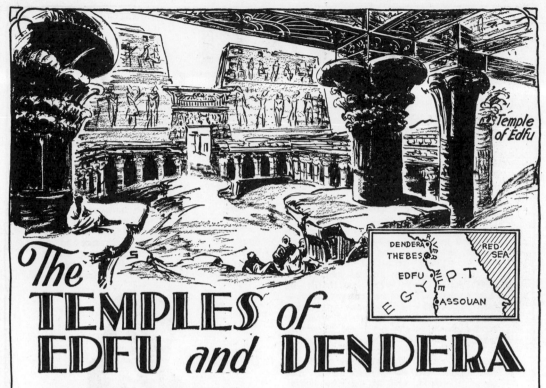

Temple of Edfu

The TEMPLES of EDFU and DENDERA

THE Temple of Edfu, dedicated to the falcon-god, Horus, is the most perfect now standing in Egypt, for though the brilliant painting of the interior is dimmed by the centuries, the sculptured vestibules, the stone facades pierced to hold flagpoles with gay pennons, the lofty pillared corridors are well-preserved. One wall portrays stirring battles between Horus, pictured divinely, and his traditional enemy, Set, shown as a hippopotamus or pig. The roof was flat, as in all Egyptian temples, and here each September at high Nile the king and queen acted as Horus and Isis in a ceremony in which an unfortunate, cast as Set, was actually slain. The inner shrine was sacred to human fertility, worshipped under the god Min of Koptos and the goddess Hathor of Dendera.

Hathor was housed in a beautiful temple at Dendera, modelled after the most splendid Egyptian mansions, with high walls for privacy, dark spacious dwelling rooms made cool and dim by the absence of large windows, and a flat roof where one took the air in the evening.

Once a year her image was placed on a sacred barge and escorted by a flotilla up the Nile, to meet the image of the god of Edfu borne by his followers. Then in the temple at Edfu there followed days of rites and pomp, before Hathor returned to Dendera for another twelve months.

Temple of Dendera

The PHAROS of Alexandria

ONE of the Seven Wonders of the World was the great lighthouse built on the Island of Pharos, that natural breakwater in the harbor of Alexandria, which Alexander the Great foresaw would become the important connection between the East and the West of the Ancient World.

It was a mighty tower, 1000 cubits high, built in many stories, with an outer winding stair up which beasts of burden ascended to the top, bearing fuel for the beacon fire which blazed in a great lantern surrounded by reflecting mirrors arranged to make the light visible 100 miles, and in the daytime to reveal ships approaching Egypt before they were perceptible to the eye.

It was built of finest stone, with pillars and galleries and ornaments of marble, on which, so they say, the architect Sostratus engraved his own name in durable characters, while he wrought a frail memorial to Ptolemy, his master, in the ephemeral cement coating.

This magnificent and unusual tower gave a suitable first impression of the gorgeous city of Alexandria, which, designed in the form of a Macedonian cloak, spread 80 furlongs (15 miles) in every direction. It contained 400 temples, 4000 palaces 400 public baths, and 1200 shops for the sale of vegetables only. Its two broad main thoroughfares were adorned with stately colonnades. The lighthouse of Pharos guided the traffic of the world into this busy port.

An Imaginative Reconstruction.

Isle of Pharos
LIGHT-HOUSE
MED. SEA
Canopic Gate
Canopic Canal
LAKE MAREOTIS
ANCIENT ALEXANDRIA

The TEMPLES of PHILAE

Pharaoh's Bed

THE Island of Philae stands with its burden of columned temples near the First Cataract of the Nile. These turbulent rapids have always presented an engineering problem to Egypt. As early as the Sixth Dynasty a pharaoh ordered five canals dug around the cataract, so that he might transport granite from the quarries near by for temples and pyramids. A regiment of negroes cut down whole forests which then grew on those banks and were thick enough to shelter elephants, and built the canals and the boats to navigate them. Now the modern Assouan Dam floods the section, including the Island of Philae, for five months of the year.

At low water the beautiful temples may be visited. They are comparatively recent for Egypt, most of them dating later than 670 B.C. and many of the finest being the work of the Romans. The most famous of these is inappropriately called "Pharaoh's Bed," a rectangular columned temple begun by Augustus Cæsar and finished by Trajan. This typically square Roman architecture stands immediately beside the essentially Egyptian slanting pylons which flank the entrance to the "Birth House," whose ancient bas-reliefs show Ptolemy VIII offering himself to Horus, Isis, and Osiris, the main "good" gods of his day.

Thus this sacred island holds on its small surface the evidences of two periods of Egyptian history, the Ptolemaic and the Roman, and both are submerged annually and with like irreverence by the engineering which preserves the life of modern Egypt.

The GREAT PYRAMID of EGYPT

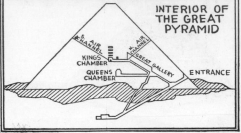

INTERIOR OF THE GREAT PYRAMID

S. AIR CHANNEL

N. AIR CHANNEL

KINGS CHAMBER

GREAT GALLERY

QUEENS CHAMBER

ENTRANCE

THREE thousand years before the birth of Christ there lived in Egypt King Cheops, who resolved to rear himself a tomb which should out-live time. So at Gizeh he built the Great Pyramid, its base covering thirteen acres, its apex soaring 482 feet in the air, 50 feet higher than the dome of St. Peter's at Rome.

This tremendous structure was built of huge blocks of stone, 40 cubic feet in size, which were hauled from quarries miles away across the Nile. Thousands of slaves wore out their lives toiling to drag those giant blocks across the hot sands, driven till they dropped by the stinging lashes of overseers. The relics of long, low barracks where these wretches sank exhausted at night may still be seen near the pyramid.

Through intricate subterranean passages and secret channels the way led to the very center of the vast pile, where were hidden the chambers of the King and Queen, the royal sarcophagi, and blind doors through which the souls were to exit, taking food and jewels for the journey to the next world.

The exterior was originally of highly polished stone, for Cheops planned that only the eagle and the serpent might reach the peak of his pyramid. But time has worn away the joints and scarred the walls, and looters have plundered the smooth stone, so that now every year thousands of curious tourists clamber up the crude stones to the top, unmindful of the pride of the Pharaohs.

MED. SEA

CAIRO

PYRAMIDS

EGYPT

RED SEA

5

The GREAT SPHINX of GIZEH

STRETCHED out at full length near the pyramids at Gizeh lies the Great Sphinx, a huge figure of a lion with a man's head, crudely hewn out of the native stone, with pieces of masonry added to complete its form. The body is 172 feet long, the forelegs 50 feet, and the head 30 by 14. This tremendous, mysterious statue was placed there by the Egyptians of the Fourth Dynasty, about 3700 B.C., probably to frighten evil spirits away from the neighboring tombs, and to guard the entrance to the Nile Valley.

The face was originally very carefully carved and painted red, but the wind-blown sands have mutilated the features, and the coloring has almost worn away with the centuries. Mohammedan fanatics and Arab raiders have hacked it, too, thinking the Sphinx some outlandish idol.

In 1816, when the sands had drifted so that the Sphinx was almost buried, Caviglia excavated the neck and forepaws, and found close to the breast a shrine, or small temple, with inscriptions left by Thothmes IV and Rameses II, who had in turn tried to clear the sands away. The Sphinx, according to their inscriptions, represented Harmachis, the sun god and guardian of the dead.

This great recumbent monster recently has been completely excavated, but the countenance remains as inscrutable as ever, gazing out over the desert as it has for ages, and we can only guess at its purpose and meaning.

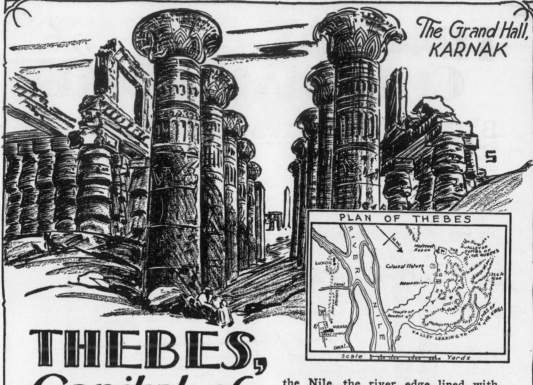

The Grand Hall, KARNAK

PLAN OF THEBES

THEBES, Capital of Ancient Egypt

THEBES, from 2100 to 950 B.C. probably the most gorgeous city of the world, is now a broken ruin, its myriad of beautiful palaces of un-baked brick and plaster trampled into fragments beneath the modern towns of Karnak and Luxor. However, majestic mutilated portions of stone temples, obelisks and pylons, and portions of avenues of sphinxes still remain, and from their vast size and elaborate structure one gets some idea of the splendor which caused this city to be called the "Mistress of Might."

It rose on the fertile east bank of the Nile, the river edge lined with quays where trading ships and pleasure barges tied, and whence the funeral processions left to "go west" to the opposite hill, which was one vast cemetery honeycombed with tombs.

The city was an expanse of brightly colored buildings, with gigantic columns richly embossed, with great sculptured pylons leading from temple to temple, with pink granite obelisks, gold-tipped—all gleaming in the sun.

The great temple of Amnon, built by a sacred lake near the Nile, was the most impressive sanctuary and so colossal that it took three pharaohs 100 years to complete one of its chambers, the vividly painted Hypostyle Hall. It was approached by avenues of kneeling sphinxes and entered through gold-studded doors of copper. Its forest of columns is so immense that human beings seem to creep through like ants. So in bygone days did the glorious Thebes dwarf the other cities of the ancient world.

TIMGAD, a glory of COLONIAL ROME

BY ORDER of the Emperor Trajan, Lucius Munatius Gallus, Commander of the Third Legion in North Africa, built there a beautiful city, where the time-retired legionaries might live with their families, and where the soldiers from the city-camp sixteen miles away might go to be reminded of Roman glory.

Timgad—then Thamugadi—was laid out with efficient regularity and designed to lack nothing that imperial Rome possessed. A main road paved with large stone blocks, now scarred with chariot ruts, bisected the town and led to the Forum in its center. Here the buildings were all of Numidian marble.

One of the most prominent citizens was Sertius, a Timgad boy who rose to a position of command and came home wealthy from the wars to present to his city a handsome market place with marble stalls, a fountain, and a portico where shoppers might find relief from the African sun.

Temples were erected to honor the gods, and also a palatial theatre, originally covered with a painted canvas canopy to keep the spectators cool. There were heated baths, and elaborate marble lavatories constantly flushed from ornamental fountains.

After Rome lost her power, in 536 A.D., a Byzantine force descended on Timgad. Realizing that the end had come and wishing to prevent the use of the city by the enemy, its people set fire to the beautiful buildings and fled to the hills, leaving behind them only that forest of pillars, now one of the grandest ruins of the world.

All that remains of the Temple to the Great Gods of Rome.

SPAIN

MOROCCO

CONSTANTINE

ALGERIA

TIMGAD

TUNIS

TRIPOLI

MED. SEA

The TOMBEAU DE LA CHRETIENNE, ALGERIA

FIFTY miles west of Algiers, on the summit of a low hill overlooking the Barbary coast, is a tumbled mound of rock, like a dome-shaped pyramid, overgrown with weeds and mutilated by centuries of misuse. This is the Tomb of the Christian Woman, once one of the most splendid mausoleums of the world, built to cherish the body of Selene Cleopatra, the beautiful daughter whom Cleopatra of Egypt bore Anthony.

The story goes back to the days of Julius Cæsar, who took Prince Juba II captive from Algiers to Rome. Then, because he pleased his fancy, he did not enslave him, but, rather educated him, married him to Selene Cleopatra, whom Octavia, Anthony's forgiving wife, had reared; then sent them back to North Africa to reign. They were highly prosperous, and the ruins of their governing city show the wealth and luxury of their lives— a hippodrome, great baths, palaces, and temples with statuary and every Roman refinement.

The Tombeau was built to hold the bodies of Juba and Selene. Its shape was probably suggested by the pyramids of the Queen's childhood, while the door panelling in the form of a cross shows the Christian motif.

Brigands and marauders through the centuries have hacked at the tomb in an effort to get its buried treasure. In 1855 Napoleon ordered two antiquarians to penetrate to the secret chamber in the center. At last they succeeded, only to find that thieves had long ago rifled it, leaving only a few scattered beads and an Egyptian pendant lying broken in the dust.

SPAIN

MED SEA

ALGIERS

AFRICA

The TREASURES of TUTANKHAMEN

TUTANKHAMEN, the boy king who reigned only eight years, was epoch-making in Egyptian history, for he restored the ancient religion which his heretic father-in-law had displaced, and moved the capital back to Thebes again.

In our day his name has become famous because his tomb, while not the largest or most elaborate was found actually intact in 1922 by Howard Carter and Lord Carnarvon. Many tombs had been discovered before, but robbers had always preceded the explorers. The antechamber of Tutankhamen's tomb, too, had been entered, but probably soon after his death, for only a few jewels or trinkets were taken, the sepulchral chamber and treasure house being left undisturbed.

So the excavators found four rooms which had been untouched for 33 centuries, containing unbelievable treasures. Pharaoh's jewelled throne, his carved gold and silver couches, stools, and chests of clothes, his alabaster jars still smelling faintly of the perfumes of ages ago, the piles of mummified food, the papyrus chair—all stood where the mourners had placed them close to the mummy, who would need them in his next life.

In these treasures we have a record of the splendor in which an ancient pharaoh was started for immortality.

The outer chamber of Tutankhamen's tomb showing blocked-up doorway to inner chamber.

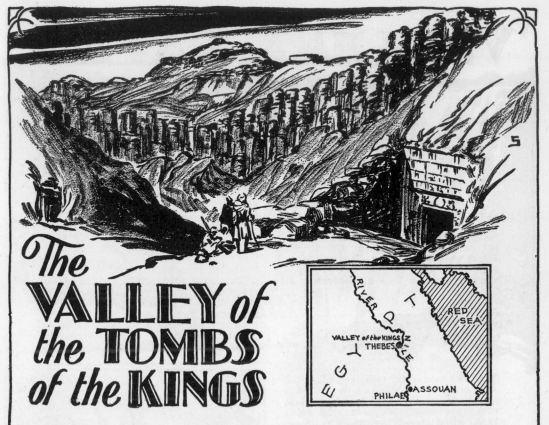

The VALLEY of the TOMBS of the KINGS

THE wealthy pharaohs of ancient Thebes at first placed their tombs close to the Nile's west bank, but robbers pillaged the jewels and funeral trappings of the illustrious dead, and it became necessary to find a more remote location. Inland a little, behind a barrier of cliffs, is a desolate valley, barren of trees, wild, and lonely. Here Thothmes I was buried by his overseer Anena, who secreted the tomb, inscribing on its rocky walls: "I arranged for the hewing of a rock tomb for his majesty, alone, no one seeing, no one hearing."

Its entrance was small, leading down steep narrow staircases to two rooms, the second containing the sandstone sarcophagus for the King's coffin. The mouth of the tomb was filled with stones and débris, and its location kept secret. Succeeding pharaohs followed this example, the entrances to their tombs being mere rabbit holes to assure safety.

Up and down the ridges of this wild valley the tombs were hidden, the later ones with more elaborate decorations and structure, with sarcophagi of pink granite and even of alabaster. The great valley became so riddled with passages and sepulchral chambers, and the earlier entrances were so obliterated, that often a pharaoh would excavate a tomb practically on top of a previous one, as when Rameses VI built immediately above the tomb of Tutankhamen. So the Valley of the Kings, apparently a deserted waste, is really the most populous city of the dead in the world.

VICTORIA FALLS

The Main Fall
from Rain Forest

5

PANORAMIC PLAN OF VICTORIA FALLS

NOT everyone realizes that the greatest waterfall in the world is not Niagara, but a tremendous cataract that was not discovered until 1855, when David Livingstone, in exploring the Zambezi River in the province of Rhodesia, in the heart of Africa, first heard its roar and named it after his Queen, Victoria of England.

The Falls, divided into four parts by islands at the brink, are more than a mile wide and are more than twice as deep as Niagara, varying from 256 feet at the right bank to 343 feet in the center. Instead of falling freely into a deep, wide basin, as does Niagara, they dash against the sheer opposite wall of the chasm with a thunderous roar, and are forced through a narrow channel, or gorge, which the plunging waters have cut into the barrier wall. So great is the pressure to which the waters are subjected as they boil through the narrow chasm, only 10 feet in width, and then into the zig-zag confines of the Grand Canyon, that great columns of mist rise perpetually, which caused the natives to name the cataract *musi-oa-tunya*, or "smoke does sound there."

The volume of water passing over Victoria Falls varies with the season, being at full flood in April and at its low mark in October. The country surrounding the cataract is heavily wooded and has been reserved by the Rhodesian government as a public park.

The RUINS at ZIMBABWE

IT IS difficult to think that the same barbaric African race which lives now in little huts of wattle and daub could ever have produced the impressive masonry at Zimbabwe. How old it is or what its purpose, no one knows. But the mute testimony of this ancient grandeur rises silently above the green of the jungle, a reminder of the days of gold and ivory traffic with Arabs and Phoenicians.

The principal building was a citadel-temple, surrounded by two great walls, often 30 feet high and 4 feet thick, made of stones painstakingly chiselled to fit together perfectly without mortar. These walls were plain, except for a zig-zag pattern of bricks at the top. Narrow staircases twist through them, the walls curving into the openings to avoid sharp corners. There are occasional round turrets rising to overtop the ramparts. It is a question whether they were watch-towers or phallic symbols of primitive religion. The courtyards were paved with rough cement, and the enclosure is a labyrinth of passages and small rooms centered about a ruined altar.

Outside, midst the remains of innumerable huts, a spring bubbles up. On the theory that natives came here to fill their water-pots, explorers have searched for trinkets which they might have dropped. They were rewarded with quantities of gold-worked articles from beads to nails, showing that gold was once abundant enough for everyday use in the years when Zimbabwe was thriving.

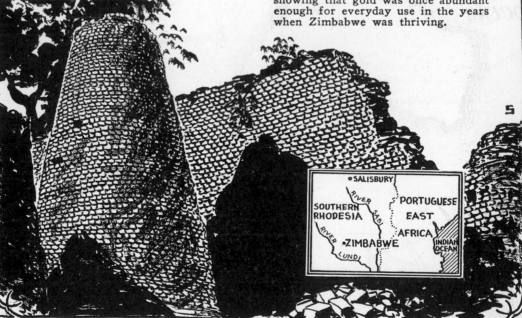

Oceania

PACIFIC OCEAN

EQUATOR

INDIAN OCEAN

BORO-BUDUR

ANTARCTIC OCEAN

SKRENDA

BORO=BUDUR, SOUL of JAVA

ON THE verdant Kedu plateau, called the Garden of Java, stands the mammoth Boro Budur, one of the largest and most elaborate temples in the world. It is a vast pile of pinnacles, turrets, cupolas, ranged tier on tier, all fantastically carved with bas-reliefs and fretwork and gargoyles, supporting high at the top a perfectly plain dagoba, which was the shrine of a very sacred relic, legend says, the ashes of Buddha himself. It is empty now; but one knows that such a gigantic masterpiece, begun in 850 A.D. and taking years of work by thousands of devotees, must have sheltered some most important object.

This great flat-topped polygonal pyramid of trachyte rests on a base 520 feet square, and is a series of circular, square, and many-sided terraces, each highly sculptured, with recesses with statues (over 400 of Buddha alone), stone-latticed alcoves, and more than two miles of remarkable reliefs which portray the complete life of the saint, unfolding as one pro-

gresses upward. When the top terrace is finally reached, the ascending pilgrim, through a weirdly carved gateway, first glimpses the serene plain dagoba which completes the temple. This symbolizes that he has been uplifted beyond human art to the pinnacle where the holiest still points upward. After the lavish detail of the structure, the simplicity of this climax well expresses the calm and poise and aloofness of that saint who inspired this incomparable tribute.